Michael P. Gadomski

THE POCONOS

Pennsylvania's Mountain Treasure

Schiffer
Publishing Ltd

4880 Lower Valley Road • Atglen, PA 19310

Other Schiffer Books by the Author:
Reserves of Strength: Pennysylvania's Natural Landscape, ISBN: 978-0-7643-4422-0
Pittsburgh: A Renaissance City,
ISBN: 978-0-7643-4923-2
Other Schiffer Books on Related Subjects:
Catskill Resorts: Lost Architecture of Paradise,
ISBN: 978-0-7643-4317-9

Designed by Molly Shields
Cover designed by John Cheek
Type set in Franklin Gothic/Times New Roman

ISBN: 978-0-7643-4924-9
Printed in China

Published by Schiffer Publishing, Ltd.
4880 Lower Valley Road
Atglen, PA 19310
Phone: (610) 593-1777; Fax: (610) 593-2002
E-mail: Info@schifferbooks.com

For our complete selection of fine books on this and related subjects, please visit our website at www. schifferbooks.com. You may also write for a free catalog.

This book may be purchased from the publisher. Please try your bookstore first.

We are always looking for people to write books on new and related subjects. If you have an idea for a book, please contact us at proposals@schifferbooks.com.

Schiffer Publishing's titles are available at special discounts for bulk purchases for sales promotions or premiums. Special editions, including personalized covers, corporate imprints, and excerpts can be created in large quantities for special needs. For more information, contact the publisher.

DEDICATION

To Peter, Benjamin, and Bridget. My wish is that there will always be a wild Poconos for you, your children, and your grandchildren to love and enjoy.

INTRODUCTION

It is generally accepted that the name "Pocono" came from the Native American Lenni-Lenape word meaning "a stream between mountains," or "the stream that runs through two mountains." But what is not agreed on is the exact original word the Lenni-Lenape used. Some references say it was "Pohoqualin," while others say it was "Pocohanne." We may never know, as so much of the Lenape culture—commonly referred to as the Delaware Indians—has sadly been lost over the years.

However, there seems to be general agreement that the "stream" was the Delaware River and the "mountains" were Mt. Minsi and Mt. Tammany, making up the Delaware Water Gap. This is the most dramatic example of "a stream between mountains" in the entire region.

Another never-ending controversy is "where are the Poconos," or "what makes up the Pocono Mountain region?" Some incorporate all of northeastern Pennsylvania, including the Endless Mountains of Susquehanna, Wyoming, Bradford, and Sullivan Counties. This is certainly too broad a definition, as the Endless Mountains have their own identity and character. Others narrow it down to all of Wayne, Pike, Monroe, and Carbon Counties. Again, this may be too broad, as very few people living in northern Wayne County, near the southern New York state border, consider themselves living in the Poconos. Others define the Poconos rather restrictively as only Monroe County or the "high glaciated plateau" as described by the Pennsylvania Geological Survey.

What confuses the issue even more is that the Pocono Mountains are not really mountains with a definite boundary; rather, the area is geologically a section of the Appalachian Plateaus Province—stretching from New York to Alabama—and an extension of New York's Catskill Mountains. It is often referred to as the Allegheny Plateau.

The Pennsylvania Geological Survey describes the Pocono Plateau as "a broad upland" composed of "tough, erosion resistant sandstones that are relatively flat lying" with "relief(s). ...generally less than 200 feet." "The low relief and relative smoothness of the upland surface results from both the flatness of the underlying rock and the scouring of the surface by glacial ice. The area was glaciated at least three different times in the past million years." In the un-drained depressions left by the glaciers, lakes, swamps, and peat bog developed.

While some define the Poconos geologically, others define it socially or economically. For this book, the area will include all of Monroe and Pike Counties along with southern Wayne and Lackawanna Counties, northeastern Carbon, and extreme eastern Luzerne County. The Delaware River defines the eastern boundary, the Moosic Mountain the western, and the Kittatinny Ridge the southern. It will take into account all of the geologically defined Glaciated Pocono Plateau Section, parts of the Glaciated Low Plateau Section, and the surrounding areas that have traditionally been part of the Pocono vacation land.

The history of the Poconos goes back 385 million years, to a time geologists call the Devonian Period. Pennsylvania was south of the Equator at the time and the vast Appalachian Sea covered much of what is now the eastern United States. To the southeast, the now-extinct Acadian Mountains were eroding. Rivers and streams originating from these mountains deposited sediment—mostly sand and clay—in the Appalachian Sea in much the same way rivers deposit sediment in deltas. Over time, the Acadian Mountains were leveled and the Appalachian Sea was filled with their eroded sediment. Over millions of years and with pressure, the sediment hardened into sandstone and shale. In the Poconos and southern New York state geologists call this bedrock the "Catskill Formation."

Starting about 22,000 years ago, vast glaciers from the north started to spread across the Poconos. This was the most recent of three glacial epics and was called the "Wisconsinan." At its peak around 19,000 years ago, the ice was thought to be more than 3,000 feet thick. As the glaciers moved across the land they carried rocks and soil, scarring the landscape, filling in valleys, leveling high points, and cutting off sheer rock ledges. When the glaciers started to melt 18,000 to 15,000 years ago, they left a changed landscape. Melting glacial runoff carved river and stream valleys. Flat lowland areas along major melt-water streams—like the Newfoundland and Greentown area—were likely glacial lakes due to the vast amount of melt-water runoff. Glacial till of gravel and sand were deposited along the glacial streams. The messic till barrens near Long Pond were formed during this time. Large blocks of ice were buried in this glacial till, melting later and forming kettle hole ponds such as Lehigh Pond and Lake Lacawac.

When the glaciers finally melted the land started to revegetate and went through several dry and moist and cool and warm periods. Scientists know this by examining the plant pollen preserved in the oxygen-poor acidic peat bogs. During this early period after the glaciers left, animals such as saber-tooth cats, giant beavers, mastodons, camels, sloths, and three-toed horses roamed the Poconos, but with the changing climate they shortly became extinct. Slowly over the next 12,000 years the plants and animals of the Poconos evolved into something somewhat similar to what we see today.

However similar, the Pocono landscape today is much different than the landscape familiar to the Native Americans in pre-Columbian times. Vast primeval forests of eastern hemlock, red spruce, yellow birch, sugar maple, and American beech covered the cool moist areas of the Poconos. This forest was so dense that sunlight rarely reached the ground. Early explorers and pioneers named it "shades of death."

American chestnut was the dominant tree species on the drier uplands. This important tree in the area's ecology nearly became extinct in the first half of the twentieth century due to a blight

accidentally introduced to North America from Asia. It only survives today because it can continue growing sprouts from its roots, which in turn die in a few years.

Majestic, tall, straight white pine trees also grew here that were later highly prized for ship masts.

But contrary to popular belief, it was not all a vast, unbroken forest. Along the Delaware River, the indigenous people made clearings for their villages, to grow crops, and attract game. Meadows from many former beaver ponds dotted the landscape, which often became the first areas settled by pioneers of European descent. On dry ridges and exposed areas frequent wildfires—produced by both natural and human causes—often burned uncontrolled, maintaining the pitch pine/scrub oak/heath barrens and resulting in a steady food supply of acorns and berries consumed by humans and wildlife.

Wolves, mountain lions, elk, and even some bison roamed the area. Migrating passenger pigeons descended in vast flocks to feed on the abundant chestnuts and beechnuts littering the hardwood forest floor. Pine martins, wolverines, and lynx found food and shelter in the coniferous forests and the heath hen was right at home in the heath barrens. Moose wallowed along lake shorelines, feeding on aquatic plants. All of these are now either extinct or exterminated from the Poconos.

At the same time there were no apple trees, fields of daisies, dandelions, multiflora rose, starlings, honey bees, house mice, and many other plants and animals that were brought to North America by European settlers.

It is also likely there were few cardinals, red-bellied woodpeckers, and tufted titmouse in the pre-Columbian Poconos. These more southerly bird species expanded their range northward during the twentieth century. There were no house finches, as this western North American bird became established in the east as recently as the 1940s. All of these birds and a few others are now common and familiar species in the Poconos.

Canada geese only migrated through the Poconos; there were no resident goose populations as there are now. Attempts to save a nearly extinct subspecies—the giant Canada goose, *Branta canadensis maxima*, which originally inhabited the central United States—were extremely fruitful. This subspecies was considered extinct by the 1950s. Because of its somewhat "tame" manner it was easily killed by unregulated hunting practices. In 1962, a small flock was discovered in Minnesota and through successful breeding and reintroduction programs, the bird is now common in the Poconos as a breeding bird and even considered a pest in some situations.

Probably one of the most defining elements of the Poconos has to be water in all its forms. The glaciers shaped the land and created our lakes and priceless wetlands. Rivers and streams were the first highways, traveled by boat or by footpaths following the water's course. The alluvial plains along the Delaware River were the first settlements, both by Native Americans and later European settlers. Commerce began along these rivers and streams as huge rafts of logs were floated to mills downstream. Local saw and gristmills sprung up along streams with either natural waterfalls or where small millpond dams could be constructed. By the nineteenth century, canals along the Lackawaxen, Delaware, and Lehigh Rivers were transporting valuable anthracite coal from the Lackawanna and Wyoming Valleys through the Poconos to major metropolitan areas, including Philadelphia and New York City. This anthracite coal was used not only to heat homes, but also to help fuel the Industrial Revolution.

In the mid-nineteenth century, northern Monroe County became a major supplier of ice for refrigeration due to the region's cold climate, abundance of wetlands that could be easily dammed to create lakes, and relatively close proximity to major metropolitan areas. This ice industry lasted for nearly 100 years and provided seasonal employment to thousands of local men.

The Lehigh and Delaware Rivers supply drinking water to millions of people downstream, while Lake Wallenpaupack supplies hydroelectricity to the nation's electrical grid. And those of us who have lived in the Poconos our entire lives, or whose families have lived here for generations, know the effects and changes on our lives and the region brought by Hurricanes Connie and Diane in 1955.

But it is tourism and outdoor recreation that may have been the biggest benefactor of the Poconos' gift of water. By 1846, the Delaware Water Gap was becoming a tourist destination for those who wanted to view the spectacular river-carved geological formations and escape the hot summer city weather. After the American Civil War, the Delaware Water Gap became the second largest inland resort area in the United States. Several resorts were operating right in the "Gap" at the start of the twentieth century. As transportation improved other resorts were built farther up on the plateau, usually on a lakeshore or along a stream. Because the clean cold-water streams of the Poconos were excellent native trout habitat, boarding houses along some of the major streams—such as Paradise Creek and the Brodhead—catered to fishermen coming to the area. Wealthy groups of sportsmen started buying large tracts of land that included lakes and streams for their private hunting and fishing clubs, including Blooming Grove Hunting & Fishing Club, Edgemere, and Porter's Lake. Although these were members only clubs, they preserved large tracts of land in a natural state.

Outdoor recreation in the Poconos and along its waterways was not restricted to the wealthy. In the early part of the twentieth century, the Commonwealth of Pennsylvania began purchasing large tracts of land at tax sales that timber companies had clear-cut and then abandoned. These lands became our state parks, state forests, and game lands. In 1902, the Commonwealth purchased lands that would become Promised Land State Park, the fourth state park in Pennsylvania. The first park facilities opened to the public in 1905. The start of Pocono tourism for the middle class began as people left the urban areas to camp for weeks at a time or to fish and swim in Pocono lakes that now belonged to the citizens of the state.

Rafting, canoeing, and kayaking have become extremely popular on the Lehigh and Delaware Rivers. Every year thousands of people come to the area to take part in running the rivers while others prefer the calmer, flat water of the lakes. During winter snow and ice provide opportunities for cross-country skiing, snowshoeing, ice skating, ice fishing, and for the highly skilled, ice climbing.

And who does not dream of owning a cabin or house on the shore of a Pocono lake or river?

After World War II, the Poconos became a honeymoon capital. Resorts throughout the region catered to young newlywed couples in love. Many of these honeymooners also fell in love with the Poconos and later returned, along with others, to escape the urban lifestyle and to make their homes in the Poconos, either as new community residents, commuters, or retirees. For several years Pike, Monroe, and Wayne Counties were the fastest growing counties in Pennsylvania.

But love requires responsibilities. One responsibility of love is to protect and nurture the object of your love. Another is to allow the thing you love to be itself and not change it into something it is not. Change is constant and good, as long as it is not controlled by personal, selfish interests. The Poconos are growing and changing, but how they will grow and change will be up to all of us and must be our responsibility.

In a 2012 study, the Nature Conservancy identified the Poconos as one of the best "climate (change) resilient" areas in the United States. Mark Anderson, Eastern Division Science Director for The Nature Conservancy, said, "these resilient landscapes will be strong enough to continue providing habitat to a wide variety of plants and animals while also serving as sources of clean drinking water, fertile soils and other important services people rely upon for survival." But he also warned, "these natural strongholds must be protected from damaging development, pollution and other negative actions, or they could lose their ability to shield nature from climate impacts."

This is a book about the rich natural heritage and proud human history of our area. It does not include every plant, animal, or natural area of the Poconos, nor every historical site or event. That would require several volumes. This book is not intended to be a guidebook, but rather an overview of the region. So if your favorite natural area or historical site is not included, be sure to tell others about it, show your enthusiasm and pride, and dedicate yourself to protecting and nurturing the thing you love so your grandchildren and great grandchildren can love it also. There are no commercial sites listed in this book. These can be found in other publications. What we see here are either sites that belong to the people through government ownership or have been preserved for the people by many non-profit organizations.

This book is for the natives and long-time residents of the Poconos—whether we are from "up the mountain" or "down the mountain"—to remind us of our magnificent natural community, our proud heritage, and the history that made us what we are today. The book is also for new residents who have yet to explore and learn about the region that you now call home and to help you understand what marvelous things are around you and now a part of you. It is also for the visitor to the Poconos—whether first time or returning—to hopefully surprise you with the wonders we have known, loved, respected, and shared with you for generations.

As the late Pennsylvania district forester Manny Gordon used to famously say, "Enjoy, Enjoy!"

The Delaware Water Gap is the most famous geological feature of the Poconos. Four hundred million years ago, as the Kittatinny Ridge began to rise, the Delaware River began cutting into the mountain faster than it rose. When the last glaciers left around 15,000 years ago the gap acquired its present look.

The summit of Mount Tammany in New Jersey offers a spectacular view of Pennsylvania's Mount Minsi and the Blue Mountain ridge, the first major ridge of the Appalachian Mountains. Geologically not part of the Poconos, it is traditionally considered part of the Poconos. The Appalachian Trail follows along this ridge.

A ledge of Devonian sandstone in Delaware State Forest tells the geological story of the Poconos. Parallel horizontal layers with lower layers that crisscross (cross bedding) indicate braiding rivers flowing across an alluvial plain 385 million years ago, depositing sediment from an eroding ancient mountain range to the southeast.

Administered by the National Park Service, the Delaware Water Gap National Recreation Area—established in 1978 from condemned lands that were purchased to build a controversial dam and reservoir—spans 70,000 acres along the middle Delaware River between Pennsylvania and New Jersey. The dam's plans were scuttled after great public opposition.

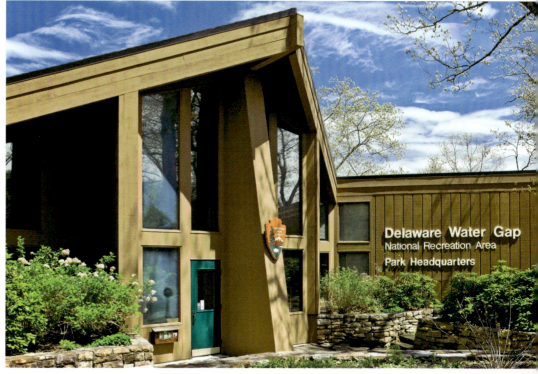

Although commonly found growing wild in other parts of Pennsylvania, native redbud (*Cercis canadensis*) is rarely found growing naturally in the Poconos. However, it is commonly planted and often thrives as an ornamental, as seen here in Shawnee in Monroe County.

A stone wall in a mature forest indicates the land was once used for agriculture. Built mainly during the eighteenth and nineteenth centuries, they were used to separate fields and pastures, or as property lines. Natural material was readily available, as rock picking in the fields was an annual chore.

These stone walls were not haphazardly laid rocks, but were often built with great care for strength and durability. One rock was placed on top of two to lock them together while small filler stones were carefully placed to keep the rows relatively level. Colorful lichens grow on the older walls.

Numerous sites in the Delaware Water Gap National Recreation Area were agricultural lands less than fifty years ago used for growing crops or as pasture for livestock. Today, the less productive lands are being allowed to return to forest, as seen here on an area of dry shale soil.

The first European settlers in the Poconos were the Dutch, who settled along the Delaware River in what is now the Delaware Water Gap National Recreation Area. The word "kill" comes from the Middle Dutch word *kille*, meaning watercourse, hence some of the current place names like Bushkill, Raymondskill.

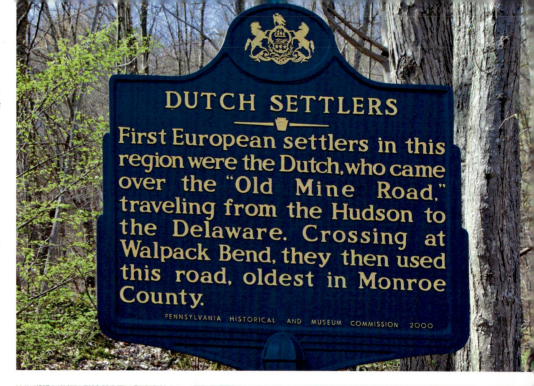

Before rural electrification and modern refrigeration, farmers used springhouses to keep milk and produce cool with flowing spring water, which is approximately a constant 50ºF. Along River Road in the Delaware Water Gap National Recreation Area, the early nineteenth century Cold Spring Farm Springhouse and Owens Springhouse are well-preserved examples.

The Eshback-Van Gorden barn along Route 209 in the Delaware Water Gap National Recreation Area traces its history as a farm nearly to the Revolutionary War, when Jacobus Van Gorden first settled the property. Subsequent owner Russell Eshback served in the Pennsylvania House of Representatives from 1958 to 1970.

A nearly full moon rises over the Delaware River at Dingmans Ferry as sunset colors the New Jersey shore. Forty miles of the Middle Delaware River passes through the Delaware Water Gap National Recreation Area and forms the boundary between Pennsylvania and New Jersey.

Spring comes to the forest along the Delaware River in the Delaware Water Gap National Recreation Area. The river is unique, in that it is the only major river in the northeastern US that remains undammed along its main stem, while thirty-five miles are designated a national scenic river.

Rising 600 feet above the Delaware River below, the forest on Zimmerman Peak in the Delaware Water Gap National Recreation Area acquires its spring foliage in early May.

Native wild bergamot (*Monarda fistulosa*) blooms in August on a former agricultural field in the Delaware Water Gap National Recreation Area. In order to prevent these areas succeeding to brush and forest and to keep them as natural meadows, the National Park Service occasionally conducts scientifically controlled burns in spring.

Found planted as an ornamental throughout the Poconos, flowering dogwood only grows wild in the Delaware River Valley and on the lower plateau. Common as a forest understory tree and rarely over thirty feet high, it also grows in the old fields in the Delaware Water Gap National Recreation Area.

The three-inch wide flowers of flowering dogwood (*Cornus florida*) appear in early and mid-May. The four pinkish-white "petals" are actually bracts—a modified or specialized leaf—while the true flower is the greenish-yellow center cluster containing up to twenty small and inconspicuous individual flowers.

(Opposite top) Marie Zimmerman's (1879-1972) summer home was built in 1912 in the Dutch Colonial Revival Style. Ms. Zimmerman was a nationally acclaimed artist in a variety of mediums, notably metal and jewelry. Her home is part of the Delaware Water Gap National Recreation Area and has been undergoing restoration.

(Opposite bottom) Upon entering the spacious and bright hall of the Zimmerman home visitors find the living room on one side and the dining room directly across. But Ms. Zimmerman, being a rather private person, entered and left her home by a side door.

The dining room in the Marie Zimmerman home has been beautifully restored as it appeared in the early twentieth century. It is said that Marie hosted only a very few select friends at her summer home.

A sitting room is in the hallway between the bedrooms in the Maria Zimmerman home. This is a feature very rare in homes today.

The graceful, curved, semi-spiral stairway leads to the second floor sleeping quarters in the Zimmerman home. Maria Zimmerman helped design the summer home in 1910 as an artistic expression of herself to create an estate with a romantic image.

The pig barn on the Zimmerman tenant farm is a two-story structure of beautiful untreated, naturally preserved softwood lumber. Three cupolas for ventilation are mounted to the roof.

The interior of the pig barn provided pens and feeding cribs that unlike many outdoor pens kept the pigs reasonably clean and dry.

In 1882, Marie Zimmerman's father purchased a working tenant farm along the Delaware River in Pike County. On this farm the Zimmerman's built their summer home. It remained a farm until purchased by the federal government in 1974. Behind the farmhouse, which is still undergoing restoration, rises Zimmerman Peak.

The Zimmerman tenant farm has two barns. The stone horse barn pictured here was built in 1847, when horses and mules were the real "horsepower" on farms. When fully restored, the farm will be used for arts and crafts, performance arts, and outdoor education.

Table Rock on Mt. Minsi, at the Delaware Water Gap, is a large expanse of flat rock. This location is an excellent example of xerarch succession, where plants are slowly invading a dry barren area. Many lichens and mosses grow here along with pitch pine, red cedar, and common juniper.

A male mourning dove (*Zenaida macroura*) in bright breeding plumage searches a grassy area for seeds and insects. Related to the now-extinct passenger pigeon, it was formally a summer resident in the Poconos, but with an increased interest in attracting backyard birds it is now a year-round resident.

The northern cardinal (*Cardinalis cardinalis*) is always welcome at every Pocono backyard bird feeder. Although now common, 100 years ago it was extremely rare in the Poconos and was mainly found in southwestern Pennsylvania. It has been expanding its range northward partly due to climate change and an increasing number of bird feeders.

(Opposite top) Hikers beginning their ascent up Mt. Minsi quickly encounter Lake Lenape. This was the site of an early twentieth century resort called Water Gap House, which was destroyed in a spectacular fire in 1915. Many of the day's rich and famous vacationed here, including Teddy Roosevelt and a young Fred Astaire.

A cedar waxwing (*Bombycilla cedrorum*) perches in a red cedar tree. They are one of the few birds whose diet consists mainly of fruit and consume red cedar berries as a winter food. They obtained their name from this habit. They are social birds, sporadically appearing in small flocks.

The 0.25-inch long bluish juniper berries on red cedar is actually a modified cone that is a favorite food for several species of birds, which in turn help plant the tree. Red cedar is a dioecious species, meaning it has both individual male and female trees.

In spite of its name, common juniper (*Juniperus communis*) is not very common in the Poconos, even though it has the largest range of any woody plant in the Northern Hemisphere. Here it is a low spreading shrub, rarely reaching four feet in height, and is found growing on rocky slopes.

Several streams in the Delaware Water Gap National Recreation Area flow through a hemlock/white pine ravine. Because of the dense forest canopy very little sunlight reaches the forest floor. This, along with the acidic soil from the conifer needles, results in very few plants growing on the forest floor.

Adams Creek, in the Delaware Water Gap National Recreation Area, carves a narrow channel through the shale and sandstone bedrock. Flowing through a steep-sided hemlock ravine forest, several species of ferns, mosses, and liverworts grow and thrive in this uniquely cool, moist environment.

A 1.1-mile rugged hiking trail along Adams Creek leads to an exquisite thirty-foot high waterfall often called Adams Creek Waterfalls. Although appearing to be an inviting swimming hole, the steep-sided walls, sharp rocks, and frigid water can be dangerous.

Any part of an organism can be host to another entire ecological community. Here the bark of an old hemlock tree supports a garden of various lichen species and moss, providing food and shelter for insects and spiders that in turn supply food for several species of birds.

The Ramirez-Nadler House—now part of the Delaware Water Gap National Recreation Area—is perhaps the first solar heated house of its kind in the United States. Originally a Victorian farmhouse damaged by fire, it was remodeled in 1942 using eighteen-foot high windows and a unique passive air circulation system.

Pocono Environmental Education Center (PEEC) occupies the buildings and grounds of the former honeymoon resort Honeymoon Haven, which were obtained by the federal government during land acquisition for the Tocks Island Dam project. PEEC is a non-profit organization in partnership with the National Park Service, providing environmental education to 24,000 people annually.

At 130 feet, Dingmans Falls is the second highest waterfall in Pennsylvania. It is also one of the most visited waterfalls in the Delaware Water Gap National Recreation Area, not only for its grandeur, but also because the entire 0.4-mile flat boardwalk trail is totally stroller and wheelchair accessible.

The Shawnee-Minisink Archaeological Site—listed in the National Register of Historic Places—was one of the few deeply buried Paleoindian campsites in the east. Excavated in the mid-1970s by American University, it revealed important clues about the climate, vegetation, and the diet of Native Americans 13,000 years ago.

Buttermilk Falls along Marshalls Creek gently cascades thirty feet over a series of terraced rocks, resulting in a step-like display of froth and foam. The waterfalls can be viewed from the Buttermilk Falls Road Bridge. Three other minor waterfalls are nearby.

Visitors on the way to view Dingmans Falls first pass slender eighty-foot high Silverthread Falls, which makes its course through a split joint fracture in the shale rock. Continuing on to Dingmans Falls, the trail passes through a mature eastern hemlock ravine forest and thickets of rhododendron.

The Delaware Water Gap National Recreation Area contains nearly 200 lakes and ponds ranging from 0.10 to 35 acres in size. One of the most popular lakes on the Pennsylvania side is scenic Hidden Lake near Bushkill. Besides fishing and picnicking, the lake is an excellent wildlife viewing area.

In 1968, the most complete mastodon skeleton ever found in Pennsylvania was discovered in a peat bog in Marshalls Creek. Estimated to have lived 12,000 years ago, it stood nine feet high and weighed between 8,000 to 10,000 pounds. It is now on exhibit in the State Museum of Pennsylvania.

Fulmar Falls, with a drop of fifty-five feet, is the highest waterfalls in Childs Park. As it cuts through the sedimentary rock it falls through two levels to the plunge pool. Due to the extremely slippery conditions and to protect the area, the waterfall is best viewed from designated trails.

Many people feel Deer Leap Falls is probably the most photogenic in Childs Park. At the top of the waterfalls Dingmans Creek has carved a narrow chute only a few feet across before dropping thirty feet. This falls can be viewed from the top where a footbridge spans the chute.

Factory Falls at Childs Park reaches a total height of twenty-eight feet in two tiers. It is named "Factory" because it supplied energy for the water-powered woolen mill that was constructed by Joseph Brook next to the falls. Before modern electricity, water power was the major source of energy for industry.

During cold winters Deer Leap Falls becomes a wall of ice with water continuing to fall inside. Although the plunge pool below the falls appears to be solid ice, the moving water underneath creates uneven ice and it is very dangerous to walk on its surface.

The Brooks family owned the land prior to being acquired by George Childs. In 1826, Joseph Brooks built a two-story woolen mill that he operated until his death in 1832. The mill operation failed shortly afterward. The original stone walls of the mill are preserved and still visible today.

In 1892, George Childs purchased scenic land along Dingmans Creek to develop a public park. Following his death in 1894, his wife donated the property to the Commonwealth of Pennsylvania to become a state park. In 1983, the Commonwealth transferred the property to the National Park Service.

The Brooks Cemetery sits on a hill above Dingmans Creek at Childs Park. Several members of the original Brooks family and their descendants are buried here. Although within the boundaries of the Delaware Water Gap National Recreation Area, the cemetery is privately owned by the Brooks family.

Some of the domestic plants that once decorated the lawns and gardens of the former home sites in the Delaware Water Gap National Recreation Area have now naturalized within the park. Here forget-me-nots (*Myosotis scorpioides*) blanket a small valley along an unnamed brook.

Common tansy (*Tanacetum vulgare*) and wild bergamot (*Monarda fistulosa*) grow in a meadow that was once an agricultural field in the Delaware Water Gap National Recreation Area. After over 200 years of settlements and cultivation, many native and naturalized plants can be found growing together as succession reclaims this land.

Two species of trillium commonly occur in the Poconos: red trillium (*Trillium erectum*, seen here) blooms in April and May on rich, moist soils. On very rare occasions it will have white flowers. Trilliums are very distinctive, having flower parts and leaves in multiples of three.

Painted trillium (*Trillium undulatum*) prefers more acidic soils than red trillium. It is usually found in forest and bog edges under conifers. Picking trilliums will kill the plant, as the leaves are needed for next year's food. Transplanting is almost always a failure and picking and transplanting may be illegal.

Rising approximately 600 feet from the Delaware River below, the Raymondskill Cliff south of Milford, in the Delaware Water Gap National Recreation Area, not only forms an impressive geological landmark, but was also the location for early silent movies featuring stars such as Tom Mix, Walter Miller, and Mary Pickford.

(Top right) Although horticulture cultivars of moss pink (*Phlox subulata*) are common in gardens throughout the area, the native variety of the wildflower is primarily found growing wild in the Poconos on the rocky shale soil in the Delaware Water Gap National Recreation Area. This perennial is a welcome sight in spring.

Many people are surprised to learn that prickly pear cactus (*Opuntia humifusa*) is native to the Poconos and grows wild on the shale cliffs above the Delaware River. These south-facing cliffs absorb solar heat, creating a very local hot, dry climate. Ecologists refer to this condition as a microclimate.

High atop the cliffs above the Delaware River a forest of stunted, twisted oak trees grow on the dry shale soil. Because of the harsh conditions, these slow-growing trees are often older than larger trees of the same species that have grown in more favorable conditions.

An old weathered bonsai-like red cedar sits atop Tri State Overlook as fog lifts from the Delaware River Valley below on an autumn morning. In the Delaware Water Gap National Recreation Area, Tri State Overlook can be reached by several trails varying from moderate to strenuous in difficulty.

Red cedars and prickly pear cactus are the two main species of plants that can thrive on the hot and dry, sheer shale barren rock face of Raymondskill Cliff. With continued good wildlife and habitat management maybe someday peregrine falcons will reclaim these cliffs as a nesting site.

Because of the steep terrain in many of the hemlock ravines above the Delaware River several areas were never logged, leaving small pockets of old growth forest as seen here near Raymondskill Falls. Many hemlocks have succumbed to the invasive hemlock woolly adelgid, but several large white pines still survive.

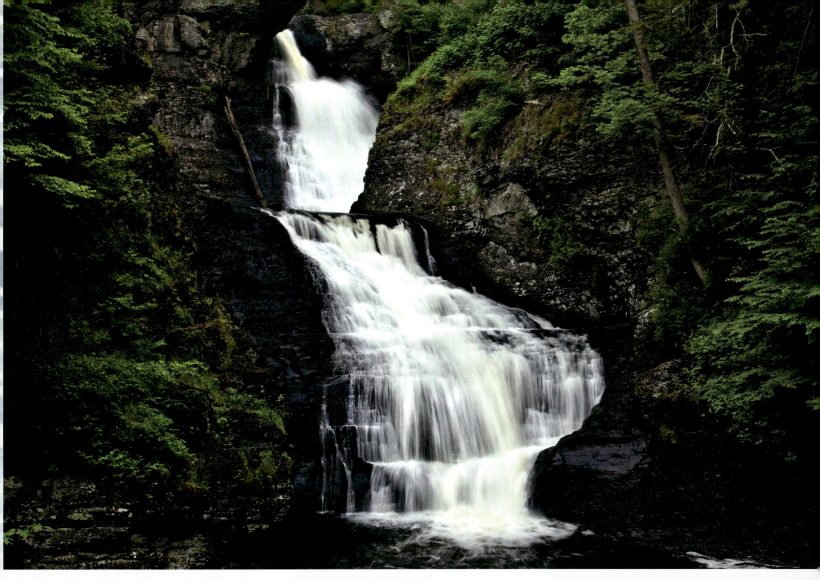

With a total drop of 150 feet in three tiers, Raymondskill Falls are the highest waterfalls in Pennsylvania and only a few feet shorter than Niagara Falls. Once a commercial tourist attraction, it is now forever protected from commercial development in the Delaware Water Gap National Recreation Area.

Due to trail erosion and the area's sensitivity, the National Park Service has wisely closed access to the lower tier of Raymondskill Falls to protect park visitors and the area's ecology. From the main viewing area, Bridal Veil Creek is seen cascading into the base pool of Raymondskill Falls.

Eastern white pine (*Pinus strobus*) can reach a height of over 150 feet and four feet in diameter. In the eighteenth century, virgin white pine covered the Poconos and was prized as masts for British ships. Masthope, in Pike County, was an area noted for its high quality white pine.

Due to a variety of habitats and soil conditions from flood plains to shale barrens, the Delaware Water Gap National Recreation Area contains a great variety of tree species. During autumn and spring, as seen here, this variety is distinguishable by the diverse colors and hues found in the foliage.

Governor Sproul's property along Adams Creek stayed in the family until it was sold to the US government during the planning to build the Tocks Island Reservoir. The 500-acre property called "Song Brook" was used as a hunting and fishing preserve. Today the hunting cabin is being assimilated into nature.

Pennsylvania Governor William Cameron Sproul developed property in the 1920s along Adams Creek that now lies within the Delaware Water Gap National Recreation Area. One of the most unique developments on the property is a rubble stone structure containing an overshot waterwheel that generated hydroelectricity for the remote private retreat.

In all seasons red maple (*Acer rubrum*) is showing off something red. In spring, before the new leaves appear, the tree is covered with millions of 1.20-inch long flowers. Red maple is now considered the most common tree in Pennsylvania because of its quick dominance after forest harvesting.

Red maple is particularly noted for its brilliant autumn foliage. Falling to the ground, the red color is quickly lost and the leaves begin to decay, returning nutrients to the soil. Those that fall in streams and lakes become food for aquatic insects, making them important in the food chain.

What may seem messy and untidy to the casual viewer, fallen trees and branches play a very vital role in a stream's ecology. Referred to by ecologists as "coarse woody debris," it provides food and shelter for fish, aquatic insects, and amphibians while improving water flow.

The historic electricity-generating Aspinall Waterwheel is built directly on Adams Falls. Although only around six feet high, the three-section falls is still extremely scenic as it cuts a smooth-sided chute through the shale bedrock. This narrow passage increased the water velocity, making the waterwheel more efficient.

While most of the Poconos' wild native orchids prefer cool moist acidic bogs, rattlesnake plantain (*Goodyera pubescens*) is generally found growing in dry sandy woodlands. The attractive 0.25-inch tiny flowers bloom during mid-summer in clusters on six to twenty-inch stalks. Up to eighty flowers can be found on one stalk.

Now growing in a forest setting in the Delaware Water Gap National Recreation Area, a large Norway spruce (*Picea abies*) with long lateral branches indicates the tree grew most of its life in an open area, with little or no other tree competition. This is called a "wolf tree."

The green frog (*Rana clamitans*) is probably the most frequently encountered frog around the water areas of the Poconos because of its diurnal habits. Its distinctive call has been described as a sound like the pluck of a loose banjo string.

Although the tiny blooms of rattlesnake plantain are very attractive, the highly decorative variegated leaves attract the greatest admiration and it is sometimes used in terrariums. Collecting plants in the wild is highly discouraged and illegal on public property. In many areas this plant has been eliminated in the wild by reckless collecting.

Most people are familiar with the common game and pan fish species, yet many are unaware of the lesser-known, yet equally common, obscure smaller fish. Usually around three to four inches in length, the margined madtom (*Noturus insignis*) prefers the clear fast rocky streams found in many parts of the Poconos.

The highest waterfall along Hornbecks Creek is the forty-foot Fourth Falls, also known to some locals as Indian Ladder. The area can be accessed by a semi-rugged hiking trail that extends two miles—partly through a hemlock grove forest—from Route 209 to Emory Road.

Four waterfalls are along Hornbecks Creek in the Delaware Water Gap National Recreation Area. Upper Falls (seen here) is more of a cascade, as it slides approximately twenty feet over the rock ledge.

Fringed polygala or gaywings plants (*Polygala paucifolia*) grow only three to seven inches high in rich, damp woods. Frequently mistaken for orchids, the flowers on this evergreen plant bloom in late spring. Generally pink to magenta in color, they rarely, but occasionally, appear pure white.

The very unique Indian pipe (*Monotropa uniflora*) is often mistakenly thought to be a fungus, but it is actually a type of flowering plant called a saprophyte. Lacking chlorophyll, it obtains nutrients from decaying matter through a complex fungal association. Not needing sunlight, it grows on the dark forest floor.

Virtually exterminated in the Poconos 100 years ago, the wild turkey (*Meleagris gallapavo*) has now made a remarkable recovery thanks to wise wildlife management, reintroductions, and reforestation. Today a common springtime sight is courting males puffing their iridescent feathers, strutting, and gobbling to attract a female.

The adult monarch butterfly (*Danaus plexippus*) feeds on the nectar from a variety of plants, although milkweed is vital in the insect's life, as the larva needs this plant to feed and obtain chemicals that make it distasteful to predators. Habitat loss and pesticide use is diminishing the monarch population.

While many people consider common milkweed (*Asclepias syriaca*) a mere roadside weed, the plant is very important and should be encouraged. The foliage of milkweed is the sole food source for the monarch butterfly's larva. Many other species of insects and butterflies also feed on the plant's nectar.

There is no better lullaby on humid late summer nights than the call of the true katydid (*Pterophylla camellifolia*). It was made famous by Oliver Wendell Holmes in his poem *To An Insect*: "I LOVE to hear thine earnest voice, Wherever thou art hid, Thou testy little dogmatist, Thou pretty Katydid!..."

The Stroudsburg United Methodist Church traces its history back to 1871, when Methodist circuit riders visited the area and held services in private homes. The present-day stone English Gothic Revival church along Main Street was built in 1915.

Several late nineteenth century buildings line Stroudsburg's Main Street, with some listed in the National Register of Historic Places. Architectural styles include Georgian, Colonial Revival, Tudor Revival, Richardson Romanesque, Victorian Romanesque, Art-Deco, Second Empire, and Italianate.

(Opposite top left) Everyone in the Poconos welcomes the stunningly beautiful Baltimore oriole (*Icterus galbula*). It is often heard singing from treetops before it is seen. Orioles prefer open forest edges, orchards, and backyards with deciduous trees. They can be enticed to visit backyard bird feeders with oranges, grape jelly, and raisins.

(Opposite middle left) Shunning deep forests, the eastern cottontail rabbit (*Sylvilagus floridanus*) favors woodland edges and meadows such as those maintained by the National Park Service. Burning to create meadows along the Delaware River has been occurring for thousands of years and first started with the native Lenape Indians to grow crops.

(Opposite top right) A beneficiary of these old fields is the beautiful American goldfinch (*Spinus tristis*). Almost exclusively seedeaters, goldfinch prefer weedy meadows that produce thistle, aster, and goldenrod. They also feed on birch and alder seeds and can be coaxed to visit feeders if nyjer or black oil seeds are provided.

(Opposite bottom left) People are sometimes surprised to see a medium-sized hawk near their backyard bird feeders. In most cases this is a Cooper's hawk (*Accipter cooperii*), whose main prey is songbirds. They recently learned bird feeders attract an easy meal. Planting shrubs and building brush piles near feeders provide shelter and help prevent attacks.

(Opposite bottom right) Unfortunately, many people dismiss pasture thistle (*Cirsium pumilum*) as a prickly unwanted weed to eradicate. Yet this native wildflower is very important to several species of desirable insects for its nectar, including butterflies. The American goldfinch feeds on the plant's seeds and uses its seed down for nest material.

Cherry Valley National Wildlife Refuge in Monroe County was established in December 2008 and is one of America's newest refuges. It is home to eighty-five rare species. The first 185 acres to be acquired—on the shoulder of the Kittatinny Ridge—contain upland hardwood forest and old maturing fields.

Growing to a height of three to ten inches, naked broomrape or cancer root (*Orobanche uniflora*) flowers in May and June in the Poconos. It is found growing in damp woods and wood margins. Lacking chlorophyll, it is a parasitic plant, obtaining its nutrients from several other plant species.

Native black-eyed Susan (*Rudbecka hirta*) is very common in wild meadows and gardens in the Poconos although it is likely it was not present here in pre-Columbian times. Botanists believe that it was native only to the prairies of central North America and "immigrated" to the northeast in the mid-nineteenth century.

As the spring sun warms the Pocono fields and meadows in May, the white blooms of wild common strawberry (*Fragaria virginiana*) appear. Native to North America, it is found in all states and throughout Canada. Numerous species of insects feed on the plant's nectar while pollinating the flower.

About a month after wild common strawberry blooms the half-inch round fruit ripens. It was this species that was bred to become the familiar domestic strawberry. The fruit of the wild variety is the sweeter of the two, but is difficult to find because numerous birds and mammals relish them.

Twenty-foot Lower Winona Falls is the second protected waterfalls in Lehman Township Community Park. It was saved from becoming a housing development by township supervisors in 2004. Three more waterfalls that were part of "Winona Five Falls" are on private property upstream and are not accessible to the public.

Saw Creek—an exceptional trout stream—runs through Lehman Township Community Park and the Winona Falls group. "Winona" is said to be the name of a Lenape princess whose legend says took her life here by jumping off the cliffs because her tribe declared war on her lover's tribe.

Once part of a commercial tourist attraction called "Winona Five Falls," later an amusement park, the Pocono Renaissance Faire, and the Pike County Agricultural Fair, this scenic area is now a public township park. Thirty-two-foot high Upper Falls (seen here) is one of two waterfalls in the park.

Just outside Milford sits the Victorian Charles S. Peirce House. Peirce (1839-1914) was a famous philosopher, physicist, and mathematician and a cofounder of the ground-breaking philosophy of pragmatism. The building is now the office for the Delaware Water Gap National Recreation Area's Division of Research & Resource Management.

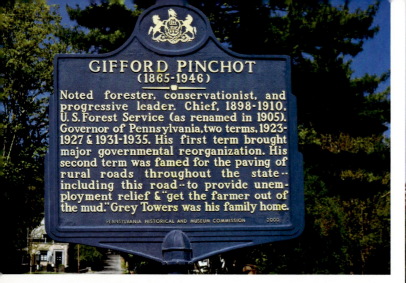

A historical plaque in Milford honors the legacy of Gifford Pinchot, credited as the founder of American conservation. He said, "Conservation means the wise use of the earth and its resources for the lasting good of men" and "The earth and its resources belong of right to its people."

The library at Grey Towers is conveniently off to the side of Governor Pinchot's office. This provided an area for relaxation, research, and to meet and converse with visitors and guests. Besides entertaining visiting business and state dignitaries, the Pinchots were well known for their community hospitality.

Regularly scheduled guided tours are conducted of the interior of Grey Towers. Upon entering the spacious mansion, visitors are greeted with a Colonial Revival fireplace decorated with various stuffed animals and a wooden panel painting. The interior appears today much as it did when the Pinchot family was in residence.

Grey Towers in Milford was built in 1886 by
James Pinchot, father of Gifford Pinchot, the first
chief of the US Forest Service and twice
governor of Pennsylvania. It served as the
family's home until 1963, when Gifford's son
donated the mansion and grounds to the US
Forest Service.

"GREY TOWERS"
GIFFORD PINCHOT HOME

HAS BEEN DESIGNATED A
REGISTERED NATIONAL
HISTORICAL LANDMARK

THIS SITE POSSESSES NATIONAL SIGNIFICANCE
IN COMMEMORATING THE HISTORY OF THE
UNITED STATES OF AMERICA
1963

THIS SITE ADMINISTERED BY
FOREST SERVICE
U.S. DEPARTMENT OF AGRICULTURE

NATIONAL HISTORIC LANDMARK PROGRAM
ADMINISTERED BY
HERITAGE CONSERVATION AND RECREATION SERVICE
UNITED STATES DEPARTMENT OF INTERIOR

On September 24, 1963, President John F. Kennedy made the formal dedication of the new Pinchot Institute for Conservation Studies. Normally peaceful Milford was swarming with Secret Service, dignitaries, and media that day. Grey Towers is now a US National Historic Site, the only one under the US Forest Service.

The small but efficient office of Governor Pinchot is in one of the front towers of the house. Here he conducted much of his business when at home. The office also contained memorabilia of his travels and adventures, in addition to samples of various wood and fishing reels.

Governor Pinchot's bedroom contains pieces of artwork he collected, as well as photographs of family and acquaintances. A writing desk provided a place for correspondence. But Gifford Pinchot loved the outdoors, and it is said he would often drag his mattress outdoors to sleep under the stars.

The historic Pike County Courthouse along Broad Street in Milford is listed on the National Register of Historic Places. Built in 1873 to replace the Old Stone Courthouse, it is a two and a half story brick building in the Second Empire architectural style featuring a projecting front and square cupola.

The Columns in Milford is home to the Pike County Historical Society. Most notable among the many artifacts on exhibit in the society's museum is the bloodstained "Lincoln Flag" that was draped over President Abraham Lincoln's body after he was assassinated in Ford's Theatre in Washington, DC, in 1865.

Milford has one of the largest collections of historical buildings in the Poconos. Several built in the nineteenth and early twentieth centuries are listed on the National Register of Historic Places. The Milford Historic District has a variety of late Victorian architecture, including mid- to late-nineteenth and twentieth Century Revivals.

The First Presbyterian Church in Milford dates back "as an evangelistic outreach among logging families in the newly settled town of Milford, holding its first formal service of Worship several years later on September 25, 1825." The present stone church built in 1874 has a congregation of over 500 members today.

In 1867 Louis Fauchère, master chef at New York's famous Delmonico's Restaurant, moved permanently to Milford to manage Hotel Fauchère, which was a summer hotel since 1852. Although locally known as "the crazy Frenchman," his creative cuisine and accommodations brought wide acclaim. Guests included presidents, governors, famous artists, and performers.

Historic Forest Hall, built in 1906 in the French Normandy style, is along Broad Street in Milford. The Pinchot family intended the building to be commercial shops and classrooms for Yale University's Forestry School on the second floor. Today the stone building houses antique stores and galleries.

In recent years Milford has developed a reputation in large metropolitan areas as being a very upscale trendy town with its art galleries, antique shops, sidewalk cafes, unique clothing stores, and numerous festivals, including the famous annual Black Bear Film Festival.

In 1824 Cyrille Pinchot, grandfather of Gifford Pinchot, built this house on Broad Street in Milford. It served as the family home until Grey Towers was built in 1886. The Pinchot family donated the Greek Revival/Neo Classic building to the community in 1924, and it is now the Milford Community House.

Found from Maine to Georgia, pitch pine is said to make its best growth throughout its entire range in Pike County, Pennsylvania. Pitch pine is a dominant tree on the glacial till soils found in Monroe County, often forming "pine barrens" similar to the famous New Jersey Pine Barrens.

The distinctive and beautiful reddish-brown bark of pitch pine (*Pinus rigida*), with its broad flattop ridges, is unlike any other tree bark in the Poconos. This thick bark helps protect the tree's sensitive cambium layer from heat, making pitch pine a common early successor after forest fires.

Savantine Falls—hidden in the Delaware State Forest in Pike County—drops forty feet into Savantine Creek before joining Sawkill Creek. There are no trails to this isolated location and a bushwhack hike is required to reach the falls.

Matamoras, in Pike County, sits below Heater Hill, rising approximately 350 feet above the Delaware River. It is the easternmost point in Pennsylvania and according to the US Census Bureau is part of the Greater New York City Metropolitan area while being the gateway to the Poconos and two national park units.

Like many areas along the Upper Delaware River, Stairway Wild Area was the site of intensive high quality bluestone mining during the nineteenth century. The flat sheet-like feldspathic sandstone was quarried and shipped by canal boats and later railroads to major metropolitan areas—especially NYC—for building material.

One factor that made bluestone mining in the area practical was that the high quality stone was already near the surface. The area had been scraped bare by glaciers over 12,000 years ago, leaving little soil. Some of these areas are now covered with a thick layer of fruticose lichens.

The group of lichens known as "fruticose" is named for their shrub-like appearance, such as this reindeer lichen (*Cladina rangiferina*), a basic food for northern reindeer. Lichens are "dual organisms" composed of two plants: a fungus and an algae living together for mutual benefit. Scientists call this "symbiosis."

Thirteen-acre Stairway Lake lies at the heart of the 2,882-acre Stairway Wild Area in Delaware State Forest. This remote lake—once a private club—can only be reached after a one and a half mile hike. A seasonal waterfall that drops forty-five feet in several tiers is downstream from the lake.

The transition stage between forest and wetland meadow is seen here at an abandoned beaver pond in the Stairway Wild Area. The dead tree trunks will eventually fall and decay. In the meantime, these dead tree trunks serve an important role as nesting sites for cavity nesting birds.

Forty-acre Colby Pond, on 2,715-acre State Game Lands 316, contains bog-like islands. Once belonging to cocaine smuggler Frederick Luytjes, the $2.8 million property (1990 value) was seized by federal drug agents upon his conviction. The largest seizure of drug-related property at the time now belongs to the citizens of Pennsylvania.

The eastern bluebird (*Sialia sialis*) is a cavity nesting bird that frequents fields, meadows, and woodland edges. When non-native competing birds like starlings and house sparrows became established, bluebird populations plummeted, yet in the Poconos they held their own, finding little competition in the wild meadow near abandoned beaver ponds.

One of the rarest native wildflowers in the Poconos and all of Pennsylvania is fringed gentian (*Gentianopsis crinita*). Its numbers have been greatly reduced, mainly from habitat loss. Flowering in mid-September, it is one of the last plants to bloom. The flower petals open only during days of sunshine.

Similar to the more familiar closed gentian, the native narrow-leaved gentian (*Gentiana linearis*) is very much at home in the Poconos, as it prefers the cooler mountain climate and moist soil. The blue or purple flower petals remain closed or nearly closed when the plant blooms in late summer.

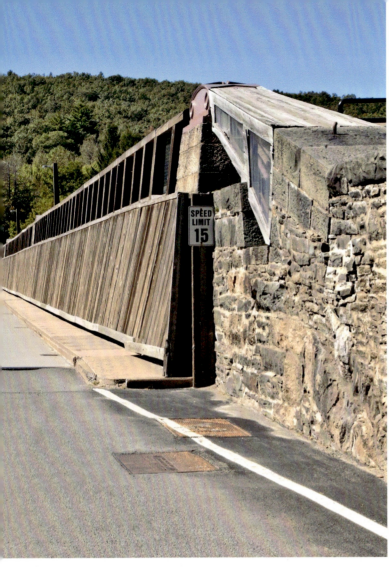

The 4.7 to 6.7-inch long northern slimy salamander (*Plethodon glutinosus*), although common in the Poconos, is rarely seen, as it prefers a reclusive lifestyle in rocky woodland ravines beneath stones and decaying logs. This harmless creature is capable of excreting a sticky, glue-like substance from its skin that discourages predators.

The Zane Grey Museum in Lackawaxen was the home of writer Zane Grey, "Father of the Western Novel." Owned by the National Park Service as part of the Upper Delaware Scenic and Recreational River, rangers provide self-guided tours of the home and display memorabilia of America's most celebrated Western novelist.

Roebling's Delaware Aqueduct (Roebling Bridge) spans the Upper Delaware River at Lackawaxen. John A. Roebling of Brooklyn Bridge fame designed the 535-foot long aqueduct in 1847 as part of the Delaware & Hudson Canal. Large icebreakers on the upriver side protect the bridge during the winter and spring ice flows.

The Roebling's Delaware Aqueduct was constructed to hold water to float canal boats over the busy river. When the canal closed in 1898 the aqueduct was converted to a private toll bridge. The National Park Service purchased the bridge in 1980 and began restoring it to its original design.

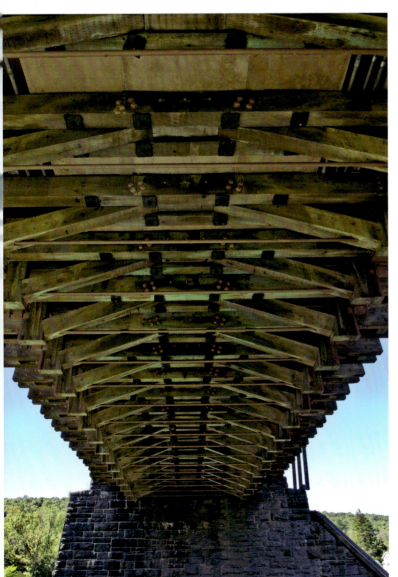

During the restoration of Roebling's Delaware Aqueduct by the National Park Service, Roebling's original plans and specifications were used. Today—except for the features to transport motor vehicle traffic—the bridge looks just as it did in the nineteenth century during the canal's heyday.

On a hillside in New York State near where Roebling's Delaware Aqueduct now sits, the American Revolutionary War Battle of Minisink was fought. The battle was a decisive British victory against the poorly trained and ill-equipped colonial militia. An unknown solider from the battle is buried in Lackawaxen.

The Lackawaxen River is not only a major wintering area for the bald eagle (*Haliaeetus leucocephalus*), but also several nesting pairs are found along its course. Once facing extinction, the symbol of the United States has made a remarkable recovery due to certain pesticide bans and modern wildlife management practices.

Honesdale was the beginning of the historic 108-mile D&H Canal. Coal from the Lackawanna Valley reached Honesdale by a gravity railroad system and then transferred to canal boats that were pulled by mules to Kingston, NY. Here the coal was shipped on barges down the Hudson River to New York City.

Founded in 1998 by Lori McKean, The Eagle Institute—a non-profit organization—provides education on eagle behavior and habitat. Now part of the Delaware Highlands Conservancy, the institute offers guided eagle observation tours along with interpretive displays and programs at their volunteer staffed Lackawaxen office during the winter months.

The Lackawaxen River flows over thirty-one miles from Prompton to the Delaware River at the village of Lackawaxen. Along most of its route relics of the historic D&H Canal are still visible. In 2010, it was designated "River of the Year" by the Pennsylvania Department of Conservation and Natural Resources.

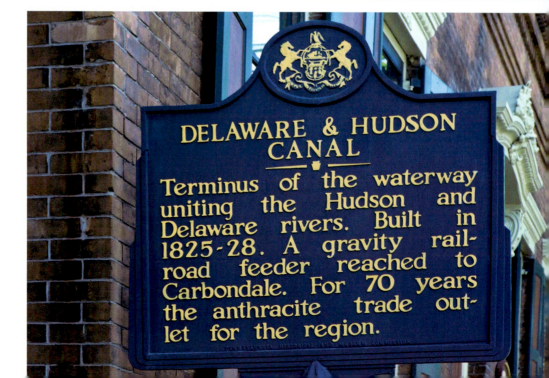

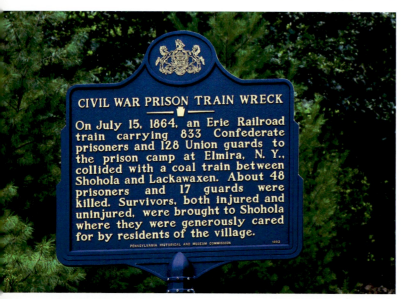

CIVIL WAR PRISON TRAIN WRECK

On July 15, 1864, an Erie Railroad train carrying 833 Confederate prisoners and 128 Union guards to the prison camp at Elmira, N. Y., collided with a coal train between Shohola and Lackawaxen. About 48 prisoners and 17 guards were killed. Survivors, both injured and uninjured, were brought to Shohola where they were generously cared for by residents of the village.

PENNSYLVANIA HISTORICAL AND MUSEUM COMMISSION   1992

Vanderbeek Farm and Equestrian Center just outside Hawley shows great local and national pride with one of their barn's paint designs.

One of the greatest train wrecks during the Civil War occurred in Pike County near Shohola, at a place called "King and Fuller's Cut." Union Guard Frank Evans described the crash scene: "The two locomotives were raised high in the air, face-to-face against each other, like giants grappling..."

The Shohola Township Museum is housed in a former 1949 Reading Penn Central caboose. Here the Shohola Railroad and Historical Society has a museum of local and railroad history, along with a tourist information center. The museum is open to the public and free of charge during the summer months.

Although a countless number of water-powered mills operated throughout the Pocono region during the nineteenth and early twentieth century, virtually all are gone and nearly forgotten. Today attractive decorative water wheels are found scattered in the area, as seen here near Blooming Grove in Pike County.

In addition to providing excellent nesting and migrating habitat for waterfowl, Shohola Lake was instrumental in the return of the bald eagle to not only the Poconos, but also the northeast. It was one of the first and important hatching sites for raising and releasing juvenile bald eagles.

Originally known as Adams Flats, present Shohola Lake was created in 1967 by damming Shohola Creek on State Game Lands 180 to form the 1,137-acre impoundment. The long, narrow, shallow lake has a mean depth of 4.9 feet and was developed to enhance waterfowl production in the area.

The mallard (*Anas platyrhynchos*) is undoubtedly the most common duck in the Poconos and indeed, the Northern Hemisphere, often becoming semi-tame in some areas. It is now more common here than in pre-Columbian times, as it expanded its range and increased its numbers as the land was cleared for agriculture.

The American wigeon (*Anas americana*) is frequently found on the Poconos' rivers, lakes, and ponds during the spring and fall migration, yet rarely in summer and winter. It was originally called "baldpate" due to the white crown patch on top of the male's head.

At the end of Shohola Creek Gorge a beautiful wild small pond around an acre in size is found. The force of the rushing water through the gorge dredged up gravel and stones from the creek's bottom and deposited it at the end of the pool, forming a natural dam.

One of the most popular waterfalls in Pike County for both sightseers and fishermen is Shohola Falls on State Game Lands 180. Here Shohola Creek drops over a series of ledges, first cascading sixty feet, then dropping ten feet more into the plunge pool in Shohola Creek Gorge.

Eastern hemlock, rhododendron, mosses, and ferns cling to the precipitous steep walls of Shohola Creek Gorge, as do many of the rocks that are slowly creeping downhill. The area supports a Canadian Life Zone and is a noted birding location.

The unusual Shohola Creek Gorge runs through an eighty-foot deep, vertical rock wall block fault on State Game Lands 180 in Pike County. Mostly inaccessible and with rather slippery conditions, the gorge is approximately 1,800 feet long. The rock structure is the Devonian age Catskill Formation.

Beginning at Bruce Lake in the Delaware State Forest, Shohola Creek flows for twenty-nine miles through forest, wetlands, and lakes before joining the Delaware River near the village of Shohola. The name Shohola is believed to be a Lenape word for "meek or faint" or "peaceful or tranquil."

On State Game Lands 183 in Pike County, Decker Creek flows through Decker Hollow. At 875 feet, it is more than 525 feet lower than the surrounding ridges. Cold air descends into this valley, making it a "frost pocket." It is home to balsam firs and snowshoe hares.

Amphibians in the Poconos migrate to vernal pools to breed during the first warm spring rains. Because these pools hold water only seasonally they cannot support fish and other predators of amphibian larva, making them vital for dwindling amphibian populations. Development and off-road vehicles have depleted vernal pond numbers.

The tiny 1.75-inch long gray treefrog (*Hyla versicolor*) is a master at camouflage, changing quickly from green to brown to gray to match its surroundings. Their mating call is often heard high in the treetops. Renowned Pocono naturalist John Serro noted a large number of these frogs in Decker Hollow.

The American toad (*Bufo americanus* [aka, *Anaxyrus americanus*]) needs water to breed and for larva development, yet adults spend most of their life on land. It is impossible to develop warts by handling a toad, however, external skin glands secrete a poisonous substance that protects the toad from some predators.

Billings Pond, on State Game Lands 180, was originally a small human-made impoundment. Now this beaver dam-enhanced wetland is vital for aquatic wildlife and even bald eagles. Rare capitate spike-rush (*Eleocharis olivacea*), which is on the Pennsylvania Natural Hertiage Program Watch List, is known to grow here.

Spotted salamanders (*Ambystoma maculatum*) spend most of their lives in woodland leaf litter, except for rainy spring nights when they migrate to breeding vernal pools. During this migration millions are killed crossing highways. The National Park Service closes River Road during these migrations to protect these and other amphibians.

Swamp rose (*Rosa palustris*) grows on the shore of some of the Poconos' lakes and wetlands. It prefers slightly acidic, moist soils. The light pink, one to two-inch diameter flowers bloom in mid-summer. The plant is propagated by several species of birds eating the rose hips and spreading the seeds.

Besides humans, no other animal changes the natural landscape more than beavers, with their dams that flood woodlands to create ponds. Beaver ponds occasionally conflict with human infrastructure but for the most part are a priceless asset, not only for wildlife habitat, but also for flood and drought control.

Nearly every beaver pond in the Poconos has at least one pair of wood ducks (*Aix sponsa*). Wood ducks nest in hollow trees and at one time were feared to be on the verge of extinction. However, with the comeback of beavers new habitat was created for the bird's survival.

A beaver pond off Big Egypt Road in the Delaware Water Gap National Recreation Area is an excellent location to observe wildlife. The area is designated an Important Bird Area. The trees that drowned by flooding are not wasted, but are used by several bird species for nesting and roosting.

Beaver lodges are a common sight in many Pocono aquatic areas. Mistakenly called a beaver dam by some, the lodge is used for shelter and a place to raise their young. In addition to the dome-shaped lodge seen here, some beavers will construct bank burrows, especially in deep-water areas.

Over time beavers may abandon their pond for several reasons. The dams will slowly fail and the pond will drain. In a few years a moist meadow will develop, adding diversity to the environment, as seen here along Kistler Run, on State Game Lands 127. Eventually a forest will return.

The Wayne County Historical Society purchased Lock 31 House in 2001 after already owning a mile of the former D&H Canal. The society is restoring the building as a living history museum. It is now open to the public during scheduled events. The old towpath-walking trail is always open.

Hawley, in Wayne County near Lake Wallenpaupack, has several historic homes built by white-collared railroad employees in the mid-nineteenth century. Each year during the borough's Winterfest a one-day tour of some of these privately owned homes is held for the public to get an inside look into these architectural treasures.

Lock 31 House near the borough of Hawley was originally a farmhouse. In 1827, Delaware & Hudson Canal Lock 31 was built directly behind the house, greatly increasing its value. In 1878, Ernst A. Hintze purchased the house, received a liquor license, and opened a hotel fronting the canal.

Nesting pairs of red-winged blackbirds (*Agelaius phoeniceus*) are found in nearly every Pocono marsh. In late winter and spring they can be found in fields and backyard feeders in large flocks. They are the true harbinger of spring, arriving in the Poconos from their wintering grounds in early March.

The female red-winged blackbird lacks the bold colors of the male. Instead, she displays brown streaks almost like a large, dark sparrow. This helps her blend into the environment when incubating eggs. The nest is built low in vertical shoots of marsh vegetation, shrubs, or trees.

Another common bird found near bodies of water in the Poconos is the eastern kingbird (*Tyrannus tyrannus*). A type of flycatcher, they can often be seen perched on a tree limb, waiting for an insect to fly by and then dashing out to catch it in flight.

Hawley Silk Mill, powered by a sixty-one-foot waterwheel from the Wallenpaupack Creek, was built in 1880 and once employed 500 women in the textile industry. Listed on the National Register of Historic Places, it now serves as a Lackawanna Community College branch campus and houses professional and commercial tenants.

The original historic White Mills Firehouse was built in 1911 for the newly created volunteer department. Moved in 1999 to its present location along Route 6, it is now part of the Dorflinger-Suydam Wildlife Sanctuary's historic White Mills project. It houses a collection of artifacts and memorabilia of White Mills.

Japanese iris (*Iris ensata*) has become naturalized in some of the meadows at the Dorflinger-Suydam Wildlife Sanctuary. Blooming in early June, this iris, along with the many native wildflowers found here, are a special treat to the human and butterfly visitors to the sanctuary.

Visitors are encouraged to enjoy passive recreation in a natural setting on the nearly 600-acre Dorflinger-Suydam Wildlife Sanctuary in White Mills. About five miles of maintained trails pass by ponds and through meadows and woodlands. The trails are ideal for birding, hiking, snowshoeing, and cross-country skiing.

One of the major features at the Dorflinger-Suydam Wildlife Sanctuary is Trout Lake. Home to many species of wildlife and aquatic plants, the lake also contains an island with a scenic, mature white pine plantation where great blue and green herons can be seen roosting or feeding along the shoreline.

The Dorflinger Glass Museum in White Mills has "the nation's largest collection of American Brilliant-cut Dorflinger Glass." In 1865, Christian Dorflinger started the Dorflinger Glass Works factory nearby that produced some of the world's supreme lead crystal for the finest homes until 1921, including the United States White House.

Dorflinger Glass Museum and the Dorflinger-Suydam Wildlife Sanctuary resulted from a generous 1979 gift to the community by Dorothy Suydam. Her will stipulated her estate be used as a wildlife sanctuary in memory of her husband, Frederick Suydam, grandson of Christian Dorflinger. It is also home to the Wildflower Music Festival.

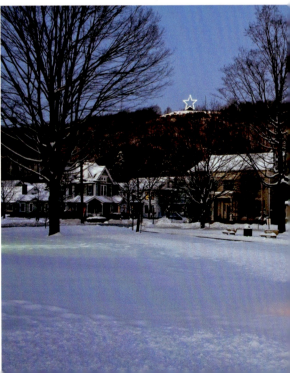

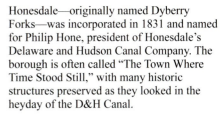

Honesdale—originally named Dyberry Forks—was incorporated in 1831 and named for Philip Hone, president of Honesdale's Delaware and Hudson Canal Company. The borough is often called "The Town Where Time Stood Still," with many historic structures preserved as they looked in the heyday of the D&H Canal.

After many years of taxpayer anger and legal and political disputes known as "The Courthouse Wars," the construction of the Wayne County Courthouse was completed in 1880 at a cost of $130,000. Today, the Second Empire architectural style structure is a source of great pride to the county's residents.

The lyrics to the popular holiday song "Winter Wonderland" were written by Dick Smith in 1934. Living on Church Street, across from Central Park in Honesdale, Smith could see the park's snow-laden trees from his home. It is widely believed that this was his inspiration to write the song.

Also common in the old-field habitat is the chipping sparrow (*Spizella passerina*). They are also common in shrubbed or tree-lined backyards. Resembling the winter visiting tree sparrow, chipping sparrows lack the tree sparrow's central breast spot and are only found in our area in the summer months.

The Eastern tiger swallowtail (*Papilio glaucus*) is one of the more familiar native butterflies seen in the Poconos. It feeds on nectar from several flower species found in meadows and gardens. It can also be seen congregating in mud puddles, where it extracts minerals that aid in reproduction.

The familiar black-capped chickadee (*Poecile atricapillus*) is found almost anywhere there are trees in the Poconos. It is common in winter at backyard feeders, where they can become semi-tame. In summer they seem to disappear, as they seek secluded nesting sites often in rotting small tree trunks, frequently birch.

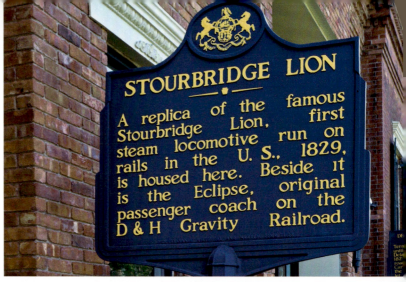

STOURBRIDGE LION

A replica of the famous Stourbridge Lion, first steam locomotive run on rails in the U. S., 1829, is housed here. Beside it is the Eclipse, original passenger coach on the D & H Gravity Railroad.

Originally built in 1904 by the Patriotic Order Sons of America, Peggy Bancroft Hall in South Sterling now serves as home to the Greene-Dreher Historical Society. It is listed on the National Register of Historic Places. Peggy Bancroft—founder of the society—is a tireless author, journalist, and local historian.

Honesdale is noted as the birthplace of the American railroad. It was here on August 8, 1829, that the first commercial steam locomotive—the Stourbridge Lion—ran in the United States. The locomotive performed very well, but the tracks were insufficient to carry its seven and a half ton weight.

Very little evidence of the former gravity railroad is left. One exception is the thirty-two-acre "Price-Simpson Wetland" near Lake Ariel. This wetland was originally a water basin for the gravity railroad engines that passed nearby. Northeast Pennsylvania Audubon Society now owns and maintains this vital and picturesque wildlife wetland area.

A full-scale replica of the Stourbridge Lion is on display in Honesdale at the Wayne County Historical Society Museum housed in the former D&H Canal's company office. The original boiler and parts from other very similar locomotives were reconstructed and are now owned by the Smithsonian Institute.

The Stourbridge Lion gets it name from the lion's face painted on the locomotive's front and from Stourbridge, England, where it was manufactured in 1828. It was shipped to the United States, reassembled in West Point, New York, and then shipped to the Delaware & Hudson Canal Company in Honesdale.

Built in 1861 by one of Honesdale's early prominent business and civic leaders, Zenas Russell, this triple brick-walled house with twelve-foot high ceilings became the editorial office of *Highlights for Children* when it was acquired by the magazine's founders Dr. Garry C. Myers and his wife Carolyn in 1963.

The historic lodge at Lacawac was built in 1903, in the style of an "Adirondack Great Camp" by the former owner, Congressman William Connell. It is listed on the National Historic Register. It has been renamed "Watress Lodge" in honor of Arthur Watress in recognition of his contributions to environmental research.

In 1966, Arthur Watress and his mother, Reyburn Watress, wanting to preserve their family estate near Lake Wallenpaupack, formed the Lacawac Sanctuary Foundation and turned over the lake, most of the infrastructure, and land to the foundation. The unique natural qualities of the sanctuary soon brought scientists to the area.

The living room of Watress Lodge, like most of the interior, is decorated with rustic trimmings, including Mission Oak furnishings, and is paneled throughout in the style of many early twentieth century rustic country estates. It is now used as a meeting and relaxation area for visiting scientists and groups.

LAKE LACAWAC

HAS BEEN DESIGNATED A
REGISTERED
NATURAL LANDMARK

UNDER THE PROVISIONS OF THE
HISTORIC SITES ACT OF AUGUST 21, 1935
THIS SITE POSSESSES EXCEPTIONAL VALUE
IN ILLUSTRATING THE NATURAL
HISTORY OF THE UNITED STATES

U. S. DEPARTMENT OF THE INTERIOR
NATIONAL PARK SERVICE

1968

The adjacent dining room at Watress Lodge is used for meetings and special programs, in addition to an eating area for overnight guests. The early twentieth century rustic style and period furnishings continue throughout the lodge.

At the heart of 545-acre Lacawac Nature Preserve is fifty-two-acre glacial Lake Lacawac. In the 1950s, Dr. Ruth Patrick of the Academy of Natural Sciences in Philadelphia, upon visiting the lake, observed that Lacawac was probably the southernmost unpolluted glacial lake in the United States and vital for scientific studies.

The Varden Conservation Area contains two ponds, native forests, meadows, streams, and vernal pools. In 1946, Dr. Shaffer started planting tree seedlings on his fallow fields. He became obsessed with the project and eventually planted over 1,000 seedlings. These are now mature trees, adding to the diversity of the area.

Visitors and new residents coming to the Poconos from urban areas are awestruck the first time they look into a clear night sky and see the Milky Way. Due to light pollution in developed areas only one in five people in the United States have ever seen the Milky Way.

In 2001, veterinarian Dr. Mead Shaffer graciously donated 430 acres of land to the Commonwealth of Pennsylvania that had been in his family since 1786. The land—now named Varden Conservation Area—is now part of the Pennsylvania state park system and is managed for passive recreation and environmental education.

Created in 1926 by Pennsylvania Power & Light for hydroelectric purposes, Lake Wallenpaupack is the largest lake in the Poconos, one of the largest in Pennsylvania, and one of the busiest recreational lakes in the state. The lake covers 5,700 acres and has a maximum depth of sixty feet.

One of the most anticipated spring wildflowers is yellow trout lily or adder's tongue lily (*Erythronium americanum*). Appearing in May in woodlands and on floodplains, the leaves on the eight-inch high plant resemble the markings on brook trout. Some years their bloom coincides with the opening of trout fishing season.

Wild columbine (*Aquilegia canadensis*) is commonly found blooming in the Poconos during May in rocky woods, or even on rock ledges. The drooping bell-like flowers contain nectar that attracts hummingbirds. When purchased from a reputable garden center or by propagating the seeds, this plant is ideal for home wildflower gardens.

Named for the trousers worn by early Dutch settlers, Dutchman's breeches (*Dicentra cucullaria*) can be seen blooming in May in rich forest soils, often on hillsides in the Poconos. This wildflower wilts almost immediately when picked and like most native wildflowers, it should be protected in the wild.

Ospreys (*Pandion haliaetus*) are the only raptor whose diet consists of live fish. It will nest on human-made platforms, as seen here at Lake Wallenpaupack. Nearly extinct by the 1960s, it is recovering since the ban on DDT, yet it is still listed as a threatened species in Pennsylvania.

Common blue violet (*Viola sororia*) is one of the Poconos' most familiar spring wildflowers. Blooming anytime from late April through May, it can be found in open woods and meadows. High in minerals and vitamin C, the flowers and leaves have been used in salads, cooked greens, tea, and jelly.

The long-spurred violet (*Viola rostrata*) blooms in May on rich alkaline rocky forest soils. The tiny three quarter-inch flowers are very distinctive with half-inch long spurs and cannot be easily confused with any other native wildflower.

Above Lake Wallenpaupack, on the edge of the Pocono Escarpment, a rather lush, moist northern hardwood forest is found off Tanglewood Trail in the Delaware State Forest. Various species of ferns, mosses, and wildflowers blanket the forest floor.

The familiar and common Blue Jay (*Cyanocitta cristata*) can be found almost anywhere in the Poconos, but prefers hardwood forest edges, towns, and bird feeders. This is a highly intelligent species with complex social systems; it communicates with both vocal and body language and has tight family bonds, mating for life.

Many people believe the dark-eyed junco (*Junco hyemalis*) is only a winter bird, common around winter feeders, but leaves during the summer. In the Poconos it is a permanent resident. During the nesting season it seeks out cool coniferous or mixed forests often close to streams like Devils Hole Creek.

The American black duck (*Anas rubripes*) was more at home in the wooded lakes and ponds in pre-Columbian Poconos. The species is now facing difficulties because it easily hybridizes with the closely related mallard, creating a loss of its gene pool. This duck species often nests some distance from water.

Along the eastern shore of Pecks Pond, in the Delaware State Forest, 330 acres of wetland have been set aside solely for waterfowl propagation, especially the American black duck. This area is closed to public access from April 1 until September 30 to allow nesting, breeding, and brood rearing.

A rugged one and a half mile bushwhack hike on State Game Lands 221 with several stream crossings through a narrowing steep-sided canyon leads to the Devils Hole, a twenty-five-foot cascade above a glacial pothole. There are many theories how the name Devils Hole came about, some versions even bordering on the supernatural.

Except for one small section, the vast majority of 315-acre Pecks Pond and its 564 acres of adjoining wetlands are within the Delaware State Forest. This shallow lake, with an average depth of only three feet, was originally a sawmill pond. Uniquely, the lake has twenty-three islands of various sizes.

Vital wetlands abound in the Poconos, making the area unique not only for Pennsylvania, but also the country. Utts Swamp, in the 936-acre Pennel Run Natural Area, is just such a site. Reptiles and amphibians are protected by special regulations within this state forest natural area in Pike County.

The summit of Camelback Mountain in Big Pocono State Park contains a unique pitch pine/scrub oak/heath barren. Once thought of as a wasteland because it could not grow commercial-size trees, we now know this environment harbors several rare and endangered species and needs to be preserved.

Magnificent views of nature can be found in places other than the grand panoramic vista. The tiny three-quarter–inch wide fiddlehead of a royal fern (*Osmunda regalis*) unfolding in spring reveals a delicate intricacy of nature for those who are perceptive and explore beyond the roadside overlooks.

Hummock or tussock sedge (*Carex stricta*) is very common in Pocono wetlands. As it grows the dead leaves fall around the edges, forming mounds up to two feet high and two feet wide. Reptiles and amphibians find shelter around the mounds while some birds use the tussocks as nest sites.

A sure sign that spring has finally arrived in the Poconos is when the yellow flowering marsh marigold (*Caltha palustris*) and the large leaves of Indian poke or false hellebore (*Veratrum viride*) appear in the wetlands. Often confused with skunk cabbage, Indian poke leaves are ribbed and skunk cabbage is veined.

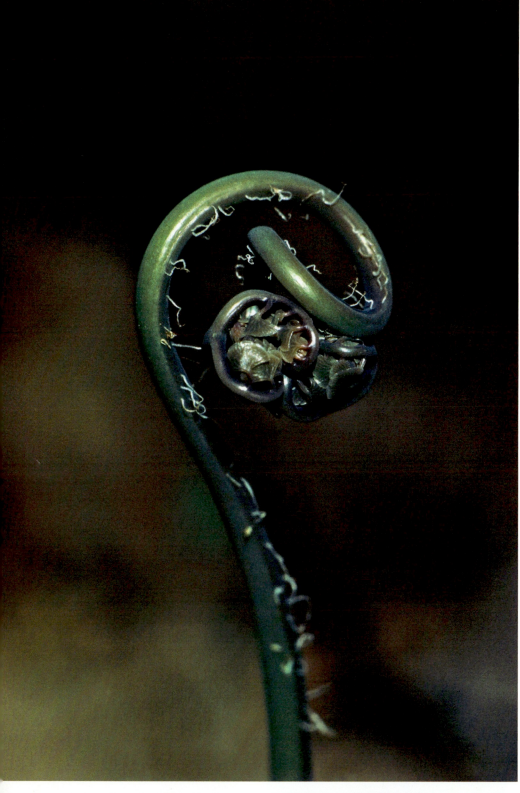

Approximately ten-acre Deep Lake, on State Game Lands 38 near Big Pocono State, is a glacial kettle hole lake. At the end of the last Ice Age a block of ice became buried in the glacial sand and gravel. When the ice melted a depression was left that filled with water.

Often confused with water lilies, water shield (*Brasenia schreberi*) grows in similar shallow water around lakes and ponds in northern Pennsylvania, as seen here at Deep Lake. The leaves on water shield are oval, rather than round like water lilies. The plant produces an inconspicuous, small dull purple flower.

Closely related to mountain laurel, sheep laurel or lambkill (*Kalmia angustifolia*) rarely grows higher than three feet. It grows abundantly in both wet and dry low nutrient soils. The flowers appear in early summer. It received its common name "lambkill" because the shrub is poisonous to livestock.

Wild lupine (*Lupinus perennis*) is not common in the Poconos, but it can sometimes be found growing on sandy glacial soil. The larva of the endangered Karner blue butterfly (*Lycaeides melissa*) feeds only on the leaves of this plant. Therefore, it should be protected and encouraged to grow wherever it is found.

Pennsylvania's official state flower, mountain laurel (*Kalmia latifolia*) grows abundantly throughout the Poconos, favoring well drained, rocky soils. The white to pink flowers appear in May and June. During the Pocono resort heyday an annual Laurel Blossom Festival was held each year around mountain laurel blooming time.

Braving the harsh elements of Camelback Mountain's summit, the stone Cattell Cabin was built as a shelter for anyone to use in 1908 by Henry S. Cattell, who owned the land at the time. The land was purchased by the Commonwealth in 1928 and is now Big Pocono State Park.

Built in 1921, Big Pocono Tower—owned by the Pennsylvania Bureau of Forestry—is considered the oldest fire tower still in service. Three states are visible from the top of the twenty-one-foot high steel tower in Big Pocono State Park on Camelback Mountain at an elevation of 2,083 feet.

Hiking two miles to Deep Lake and then following along its outlet stream (Sand Spring Run) for another quarter mile, one comes to another slightly smaller and shallower, yet picturesque isolated lake, Sand Spring Lake. This is an excellent birding and wildlife viewing area for those who are patient and quiet.

In winter, the pitch pine/scrub oak/heath barren on Camelback Mountain seems like a cold, wind-swept, desolated environment. Very few animals are visible at this time, yet surprisingly to some people the snowshoe hare, usually found in low elevation wetlands, finds a suitable home in these barrens.

Standing at 2,131 feet on the summit of Big Pocono State Park and looking southwest, the gaps along the Pocono Escarpment are visible: Dry Gap, Fall Gap, Bowers Gap, Hypsy Gap, and Popular Gap.

Often incorrectly called a "red-headed woodpecker," the once rare red-bellied woodpecker (*Melanerpes carolinus*) is now a common Pocono bird around homes and in deciduous forests. The red-bellied woodpecker is essentially a southern species that started to expand its range into northern areas like the Poconos in the mid-twentieth century.

A northern tree, paper birch (*Betula papyrifera*) is native to the Poconos and is found growing in young forests that are reclaiming the land after a clearing or forest fires. It is a short-lived tree, replaced in a few decades by more shade tolerant trees in the procession of succession.

All species of woodpeckers native to Pennsylvania occur in the Pocono Mountains. The yellow-bellied sapsucker (*Sphyrapicus varius*)—a summer resident—has the unique feeding habit of drilling small parallel holes in tree trunks to drink the sap and feed on insects that are also attracted to the sap.

The Mud Pond dugout canoe is on display at the State Museum of Pennsylvania in Harrisburg. Carbon dated to 1250 AD, it is the oldest dugout ever discovered in the state. It is believed Native Americans sunk their dugout canoes in winter to prevent damage from freezing and thawing waters.

Mud Pond, on State Game Lands 91 in Luzerne County, is a natural glacial lake of about twelve acres and contains a small boreal bog. Seemingly insignificant, the lake made archaeological history in 1935 when a dugout canoe estimated to be nearly 700 years old was discovered in the lake.

The quaking bog along the southeast shore of Mud Pond is typical of many bogs in the Poconos, with sphagnum moss, leatherleaf, carnivorous plants, and boreal trees. Decay is very slow in the acidic waters, and dead plant matter will accumulate over thousands of years to completely fill the bog.

The most common and familiar native wild orchid in the Poconos is the pink moccasin flower or lady's slipper (*Cypripedium acaule*). Blooming around mid-May, it prefers acidic soils around pines. It should never be picked and will not transplant to home gardens due to a complex relationship with a specific fungus.

The pink moccasin flower is almost always pink in the Poconos, but sometimes the rare pure white variety can be found. Rarer still is one that is both pink and white. The large pouch-like flowers are uniquely designed to be pollinated by large bees as they enter and exit the pouch.

Large cranberry (*Vaccinium macrocarpon*) is native to North America. It was from this wild plant that the domestic cranberry was developed. In the wild, the plant favors an acidic bog environment and can be found in most Pocono boreal bogs, often growing in low dense masses on sphagnum moss.

Beautiful rhodora (*Rhododendron canadense*), a native wild azalea blooming in mid-May, brings wildflower enthusiasts to the Poconos to view this rare Pennsylvania plant. Although common in some parts of the Poconos, this northern plant is at its southern limit here and grows in very few other locations in northern Pennsylvania.

The uncommon eastern dwarf cherry (*Prunus susquehanae*) can only be found on the sandy glacial till barrens. Rarely exceeding three feet in height, it has become uncommon over the years because it is dependent on fire to suppress competing taller vegetation. Controlled burns are beginning to restore its habitat.

Rhodora is commonly found in wetlands on higher elevations of the Lehigh River watershed and the mesic till barrens near Long Pond, continuing on the Pocono Escarpment to Camelback Mountain. Due to forest fire suppression, mesic till barrens have dwindled and now prescribed burns are needed to restore this unique environment.

Monroe County's Long Pond is actually a wide section of Tunkhannock Creek, approximately two and three-quarter miles long. Harboring boreal species and surrounded by mesic till barrens, the Nature Conservancy notes the area is the "only natural community of its kind in the world." The Audubon Society designated it an "Important Bird Area."

A dense stand of northern highbush blueberry surrounds the shoreline of Promised Land Lake in Crane's Nest Cove. In autumn, after most of the deciduous trees have lost their leaves, highbush blueberry puts on a brilliant show with its intense crimson-colored leaves.

The fruit of northern highbush blueberry begins to ripen in mid-July and may continue through August. It is a much sought after prize not only by humans, but countless species of wildlife. A wild native species to the Poconos, highbush blueberry has been cultivated to develop the common domestic blueberry.

Northern highbush blueberry (*Vaccinium corymbosum*) flowers in mid-May just as its new leaves are unfolding. The sweet nectar attracts bees and other insects. Growing over six feet high and favoring moist acidic soils, highbush blueberry frequently forms impenetrable thickets around the Poconos' wetlands, providing a favorite habitat for black bears.

Sucker Brook is one of six named inlet creeks for Promised Land Lake. Originating from springs surfacing in a small red spruce/hemlock forest, the stream flows for less than a mile—including through a small wetland—to join Promised Land Lake. Its cool clean water enriches the lake.

Misnomer Crane's Nest is a small, totally spring-fed wetland inlet of Promised Land Lake. Because cranes were not historically native to Pennsylvania the name is probably a reference to the common great blue heron that at times has been locally called a crane.

Between 1933 and 1941, the Civilian Conservations Corps planted thousands of trees in Promised Land State Park, including a plantation near the present-day picnic area. To protect the health of this plantation it was scientifically thinned in the late 1990s and since then an explosion of natural regeneration has occurred.

Promised Land State Park and the surrounding state forest once supported a virgin white pine/ hemlock forest before the nineteenth century logging boom. Following logging and subsequent forest fires hardwoods became dominant. However, in many places white pines are succeeding in the forest understory, reclaiming their dominant position in the forest.

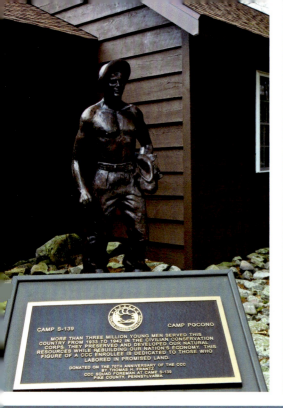

A statue outside Masker Museum at Promised Land State Park honors the men of the Civilian Conservation Corps (CCC) and their work in the park from 1933 to 1941. In addition to having many natural history displays, this museum is one of the largest CCC museums in Pennsylvania.

An early winter ice storm glazes the upland hardwood forest at Promised Land State Park. Ice storms occur when rain falls through a warm air layer and then meets a cold air layer below and freezes on contact with any surface. Ice storms can be very destructive, yet beautiful.

Another new resident of the Poconos is the house finch (*Haemorhous mexicanus*). Originally native to the western United States, in 1940, a number of caged finches were turned loose in New York state and quickly established an eastern population that is starting to exhibit differences from the separated western population.

Norway spruce (*Picea abies*) is a native of northern and central Europe, yet it has been planted widely throughout the Poconos for landscaping and reforestation. The Civilian Conservation Corps planted the magnificent Norway spruce trees seen all around Promised Land State Park during the 1930s.

While most of the shoreline of 422-acre Promised Land Lake is lined with state-leased cabins, an undeveloped cove is found near Cranes Nest. Beaver, mink, river otter, and several species of birds can be seen here. The entire park has been designated an Important Bird Area by Audubon Pennsylvania.

Dramatic stratocumulus undulatus clouds form over Lower Lake at Promised Land State Park in early February. A relatively shallow impoundment covering 173 acres, Lower Lake has supported an active bald eagle nest for several years. The Pennsylvania Fish & Boat Commissions reports the lake harbors thirteen species of game fish.

A winter sunset is reflected in the partly frozen waters of Lower Lake. Even during the coldest winters an area of open water is generally found where the East Branch Wallenpaupack Creek flows into the lake, making some habitat for a few hardy waterfowl.

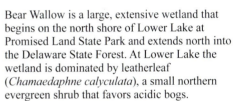

Rushes cast their reflection in the calm waters of the East Branch Wallenpaupack Creek as it flows into Lower Lake at Promised Land State Park.

Bear Wallow is a large, extensive wetland that begins on the north shore of Lower Lake at Promised Land State Park and extends north into the Delaware State Forest. At Lower Lake the wetland is dominated by leatherleaf (*Chamaedaphne calyculata*), a small northern evergreen shrub that favors acidic bogs.

An aurora borealis displays over Promised Land Lake. These auroras (northern lights) occur when highly charged electrons from solar winds interact with the earth's atmosphere. Auroras and all astronomical displays are becoming more difficult to witness as light pollution from development brightens the night sky with artificial light.

Traveling for over two miles before joining Promised Land Lake, Big Inlet flows through wetlands, old beaver pond meadows, and conifer and hardwood forests. At times its course divides and disappears underground for a short distance through loose glacial rock debris. This high quality stream supports a small native trout population.

Long shadows from the Norway spruce trees that encircle the shore reach out across frozen Promised Land Lake on a late winter afternoon. Planted by the Civilian Conservation Corps, these spruce trees are now a priceless asset to the park.

What Little Falls along the East Branch Wallenpaupack Creek in Promised Land State Park lacks in height, it makes up for in scenic beauty. The half mile trail to the falls parallels the creek, passing through an eastern hemlock forest. The location is an excellent site to observe migrating spring warblers.

Common throughout the Poconos in moist meadows and wetlands, meadowsweet (*Spiraea latifolia*) blooms in mid-summer. Growing to a height of two to five feet, the plant displays a cluster of white or pinkish flowers attractive to insects. Related to the domestic garden variety spiraeas, it is excellent for native wildflower gardens.

Rhododendron or great laurel (*Rhododendron maximum*) puts on a grand show in the Poconos from late June through July. It prefers growing in the shady forest understory in cool and moist environments. In winter, the leaves begin to curl when the temperature drops below 35°F to prevent moisture loss.

Wild calla or water arum (*Calla palustris*) is a northern species always associated with cool boggy areas and usually found growing in sphagnum moss. The Pocono Mountains is one of the few places it grows wild in Pennsylvania. The two-inch long spathe and flower usually appear in late spring.

Forty-eight-acre Egypt Meadows Lake was constructed by the Civilian Conservation Corps in 1935 and is now part of the Bruce Lake State Forest Natural Area. The lake can be accessed by two hiking trails originating off Route 390 or by several hiking trails originating in Promised Land State Park.

Once containing a virgin forest of white pine and hemlock that was cut during the nineteenth century logging boom, the 4,300-acre Bruce Lake State Forest Natural Area now contains a mixture of hardwood and conifer trees intermixed with wetlands of various sizes and descriptions, such as this small open wetland.

Rhododendron often forms impassable thickets in many places in the Poconos with their five to fifteen-foot high twisted trunks. A curse to the hiker trying to bushwhack these thickets, they nevertheless provide excellent shelter and hiding places for many species of wildlife, including the black bear.

Massive Balsam Swamp, extending southward from Egypt Meadows Lake, is a "high quality example of a broadleaf-conifer swamp" according to the Pennsylvania Natural Heritage Program. It is a true impenetrable wilderness with a dense understory of rhododendron and highbush blueberry. It contains many trees that are over 125 years old.

Glacially carved fifty-six-acre Bruce Lake, in the Bruce Lake State Forest Natural Area, has no inlet and is completely spring-fed. The lake is the source of Shohola Creek. Motorized vehicles are prohibited in the area. A nearly three-mile hike or cross-country ski trip is required to reach this pristine location.

An interesting twenty-foot high rock ledge is on the eastern shore of Bruce Lake. Composed of Devonian sandstone that formed 354 to 417 million years ago, the ledge clearly demonstrates the effect of weathering, where freezing and thawing in the rock's fractures is slowly eroding the ledge.

Another group of lichens are called "foliose" for their leaf-like appearance. Rock tripe or toadskin lichen (*Umbilicaria papulosa*) grows on the surface of bare rocks and are known as "pioneer plants" that start the soil forming process. Lichens cannot tolerate any air pollution and are indicators of a clean environment.

Many first time visitors to the Poconos marvel at a forest floor entirely blanketed with hay-scented ferns (*Dennstaedtia punctilobula*). In spite of its stunning beauty, it indicates an overpopulation of white-tailed deer. Hay-scented fern is one of the few plants white-tailed deer will not eat.

The 1.5 to 2-inch flowers of pink azalea or pinxter flower (*Rhododendron periclymenoides*) appear in May as the leaves are developing. It grows in moist woods throughout the Poconos, reaching an average height of around four to five feet. Prized for its ornamental qualities, it was introduced to England in 1734.

Gravel Pond lies at the base of Mount Wismer. Land adjacent to the pond (but not the pond) is part of the 170-acre Gravel Family Preserve. Acquired in 2006 through the efforts of local government, private organizations, and donations, it protects the area's natural resources while providing public passive recreation.

Few people make the three-mile-long journey by foot to Bruce Lake in the winter, yet those who do find the reward of solitude. As part of a 4,300-acre state forest natural area, the area is almost wilderness and is also designated an Important Bird Area by Audubon Pennsylvania.

Northeast of Mount Wismer, West Mountain—of nearly equal height—displays an autumn forest at peak color. There are no true mountains in the Poconos; rather, what we perceive as mountains are actually dissected sections of the Pocono Plateau that forms along the escarpment.

The tiny flowers of bluets (*Houstonia caerulea*) typically mass to form patches of blooms. Rarely growing higher than six inches and found in open forests, clearings, and even lawns, these delicate perennial wildflowers welcome the arrival of spring.

Nearly every winter the American tree sparrow (*Spizella arborea*) will leave its summer home in the Arctic and taiga scrublands to spend the winter in the Poconos. A hardy bird that braves the worst of Pocono weather, it favors weedy meadows and open bushy areas while frequently visiting bird feeders.

Spring comes to the hardwood forest surrounding two-acre Snow Hill Pond in the Delaware State Forest. Although this human-made pond is relatively small, it still holds a population of trout and bass. It is also a popular picnic area.

Everyone is familiar with the masked bandit face of the common raccoon (*Procyon lotor*). Originally inhabiting forest and woodlands near waterways, raccoons now thrive in almost every habitat, often close to human habitation because of their adaptability. Conflicts with humans usually occur due to human feeding or inadequate trash storage.

After a three-quarter mile climb to the nearly
2,000-foot summit of Mount Wismer in the
ninety-four-acre Mount Wismer Preserve in
Barrett Township, Monroe County, hikers are
rewarded with southerly panoramic views of the
Lower Pocono Plateau. To the southeast the
Kittatinny Ridge and New Jersey are visible.

The reflection of tamaracks and black spruce in the calm water of Lehigh Pond resembles a scene from northern Canada. The water in Lehigh Pond is oligotrophic, meaning low in nutrients and clean. It is also the headwaters of the Lehigh River, an important water source for the Lehigh Valley.

Fifteen-acre tear-shaped Lehigh Pond on State Game Lands 312 in Wayne County is one the finest examples of a glacial kettle hole lake in the Poconos. Surrounded by 3,912 acres of state game lands, the area was acquired by cooperative efforts of the Wildlands Conservancy, Ducks Unlimited, and the Nature Conservancy.

The quaking boreal bog that surrounds Lehigh Pond contains several plants of special concern in Pennsylvania. No trails access the lake and it can only be reached through a very difficult wet bushwhack. Due to the very fragile nature of the bog human activity should be kept to a minimum.

Bog laurel (*Kalmia polifolia*) grows across Canada, but is only found as far south as the Poconos. Here it is uncommon and only grows in a few boreal bogs. It resembles common sheep laurel, but unlike sheep laurel, whose flowers grow around the stem, bog laurel clusters at the top.

While mainly known as a winter resident and migrant in much of Pennsylvania, the white-throated sparrow (*Zonotrichia albicollis*) regularly nests in the Poconos. A northern nesting bird, it finds favorable habitat along the Poconos' bog edges and in boreal forests, such as Spruce Swamp Natural Area.

Tamarack or American larch (*Larix laricina*) encircles Lehigh Pond. This native deciduous conifer turns a brilliant yellow in late autumn after the deciduous hardwoods have lost their leaves. In the winter the trees stand bare until new green needles begin appearing in late April.

The cones of tamarack are the smallest of any larch—generally about half an inch long—and sit upright on the branch. They often preside on the tree for several years. Birds such as ruffed grouse and crossbills feed on the seeds. Tamaracks grow as far as the tree line in the tundra.

In addition to steam locomotives, Steamtown National Historic Site will occasionally use historic diesel locomotives for its Pocono excursions, such as this 1948 Lackawanna Railroad #664 on loan to the National Park Service from Anthracite Railroads Historical Society, Inc., seen passing the Victorian-era Moscow railroad station in Lackawanna County.

The Gouldsboro Train Station was built in 1907 by the Delaware, Lackawanna & Western Railroad (DL&W). When rail passenger service from Scranton, PA, to Hoboken, NJ, ended in the 1970s, the station fell into disrepair. It is now beautifully restored by the Gouldsboro AREA Foundation and serves as a museum.

The Canadian National 3254—a 2-8-2 Mikado steam locomotive built in 1917—makes an excursion run from Steamtown National Historic Site in Scranton to Tobyhanna. During the year several excursions are offered to Moscow, Gouldsboro, Tobyhanna, and East Stroudsburg from Scranton using historic steam or diesel engines.

The present Cresco Station built in the 1880s was used for both freight and passenger rail traffic until 1967, when it closed. At its peak in the 1930s and '40s it served up to 1,000 passengers a day, many tourists and vacationers to the Poconos.

Abandoned and falling into disrepair, restoration on the Cresco Station was begun in the 1990s by the Weiler Family Foundation. Careful attention was paid to restoring as much original detail as possible, including supports, furniture, and stained glass windows. The building now serves as a museum for the Barrett Township Historical Society.

The Delaware, Lackawanna & Western Railroad built the Tobyhanna Station in 1908. Now closed, it is used as a museum. With Tobyhanna probably being the coldest location in the Poconos, this station played a vital role in the ice industry in addition to its service to nearby Tobyhanna Army Depot.

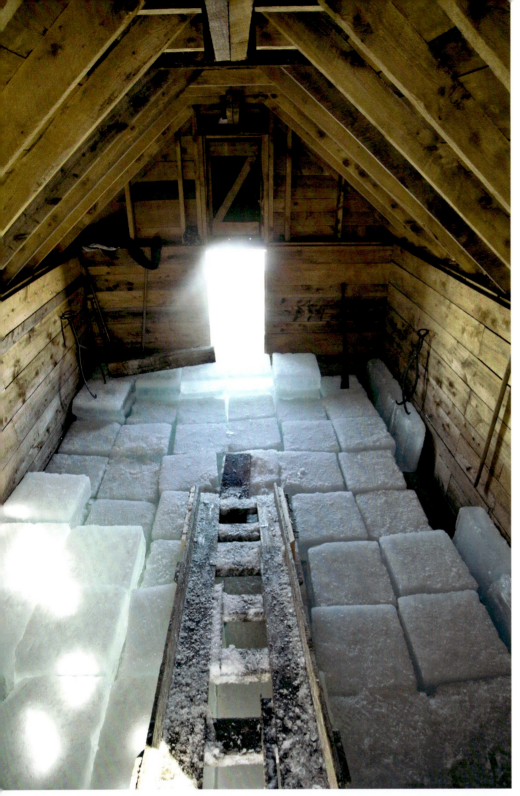

The harvest begins by cutting parallel and perpendicular grooves into the ice two-thirds of the ice thickness, forming a checkerboard pattern. Originally horses or mules pulled an ice plow to make the cut. Later, as shown here, a gas-powered 1919 invention called the Gifford Wood Ice Saw was used.

Once the ice is scored, individual blocks or cakes twenty-two by thirty-three inches are cut with a special hand or mechanical ice saw and broken from the main ice sheet with a spud bar. The cakes are then moved in large sections called "floats" toward the icehouse.

Inside the icehouse the cakes come down a ramp and are hand-stacked by workmen inside. The thick wooden hemlock walls of the icehouses were insulated with sawdust, preserving the ice that was then shipped to major eastern cities or used in ice-cooled railroad boxcars throughout the summer.

Ice conditions permitting, each winter since 1994 local residents and tourists take part in the annual Tobyhanna Millpond #1 Ice Harvest. It was the dream of the late Bill Leonard Sr. to pass along the heritage of this once important Pocono industry in which he worked as a boy.

Upon reaching the icehouse, the cakes are floated individually through a channel cut in the ice until reaching a conveyor ramp. Here groups of cakes are hoisted to the top of the icehouse. Originally steam-powered conveyors were used, but during today's harvest a tractor or actual horsepower is used.

The North Jersey & Pocono Mountain Ice Company created and expanded Gouldsboro Lake in 1895 by building a dam at the outlet of an existing lake to allow more ice to be harvested. The Pennsylvania Fish and Boat Commission acquired the lake in 1956, and the park opened in 1958.

One of the highest locations in the Poconos is at Tobyhanna State Park on Kistler Ledge at 2,215 feet. Open rocky areas found here were left bare by the glaciers. About a half mile north on private property is Hardwood Ridge, possibly the highest point in the Poconos at 2,230 feet.

Blooming in early June along streams, lakesides, and most wetlands, the familiar northern blue flag (*Iris versicolor*) welcomes summer to the Poconos. Usually found in small clusters, occasionally larger clusters can be found as seen here at Snag Pond in Gouldsboro.

The 250-acre Gouldsboro Lake is the centerpiece of 2,800-acre Gouldsboro State Park. This lake, like so many in the area, was a site for the huge Pocono ice industry. Nearby Gouldsboro village was named for Jay Gould (1836-1892), a principal American railroad developer and speculator in leather tanning.

On barren sandy soils, often the only plants that can grow are non-flowering plants like reindeer lichen (*Cladonia rangiferina*) and stag's-horn clubmoss (*Lycopodium clavatum*). Both of these plants are extremely cold tolerant and range north into the tundra of Canada.

Most of the forest surrounding 170-acre Tobyhanna Lake at Tobyhanna State Park consists of a northern hardwood forest, with American beech, red maple, and yellow birch the most common species. Between 1900 and 1936, Tobyhanna Lake and nearby Gouldsboro Lake were sites of the huge Pocono ice industry.

Damming Tobyhanna Creek where it flowed through a former glacial wetland created Tobyhanna Lake. Along the southwest and northeast shore remnants of this former wetland remain and support typical boreal bog species, including cotton grass and pitcher plants. This fragile and somewhat unsafe environment is best viewed from a boat.

Northern pitcher plant (*Sarracenia purpurea*) is one of three carnivorous plants native to the Poconos. It is found only in nutrient poor sphagnum bogs. It gets its name from the pitcher-like shape of the leaves, which vary in color from green to purple-red and are designed to collect water.

The leaves of the pitcher plant have a smooth front lip and downward pointing hairs on the backside that prevent the escape of its insect prey. Insects attracted to the color of the plant fall into the water and drown. Enzymes secreted by the plant then help to digest its prey.

The northern pitcher plant blooms in June and July in the Poconos with two-inch wide umbrella-like arrangements on a one to two-foot stalk. Because of its unique habitat requirements, the pitcher plant is uncommon and should never be picked or transplanted. Laws prohibit picking or transplanting on state or federal property.

In autumn, cotton grass is in its prime as highbush blueberry bushes take on a crimson glow in Yetter Swamp. Like many open wetlands in the Poconos, beaver activity and wildfires played an important role in their development.

Although lacking chlorophyll and dead, the leaves on young American beech trees (*Fagus grandifolia*) persist throughout winter. American beech is one of the few trees in the Poconos that can grow in its own shade, making it a climax species in forest succession.

Rhodora (*Rhododendron canadense*), tussock sedge (*Carex stricta*), and cotton grass (*Eriophorum virginicum*) make a wonderful natural spring wildflower garden in Yetter Swamp along Fritz Run on State Game Lands 127. This is sight unseen by most people due to the impassable surrounding blueberry/rhododendron thickets and boggy conditions.

A couple of miles downstream from Tobyhanna Lake another ice lake of nearly equal size once prospered. Named Warnertown Lake, it was the last lake to harvest ice commercially. The dam went out during Hurricane Diane in 1955, and the former lake bed is now reverting back to stream and forest.

The bedrock around Warnertown Falls exhibits evidence of the last Ice Age, which ended in the Poconos 12,000 years ago. The parallel lines on the rock, running perpendicular to the sedimentary rock fissions, are glacial striations or scratches cut by abrasives in the glacier as it moved across the landscape.

In some locations the glaciers left deep sandy deposits. After the nineteenth century logging boom forest fires burned the topsoil, leaving nutrient poor soils that limit tree growth. Some areas evolved into small open heath barrens that support drought resistant plants, as seen here along Tobyhanna Creek.

Tobyhanna Creek's pristine water flows through several miles of State Game Lands 127. At times it is slow and meandering while at other times rapidly cascading. Tobyhanna is said to originate from a Native American word meaning "a stream whose banks are fringed with alder."

The Warnertown Dam was built on the solid bedrock sandstone that makes up Warnertown Falls downstream from the dam site. Before dropping into the plunge pool, Tobyhanna Creek flows for several hundred feet on the bedrock, making it one of the most unusual and scenic waterfalls in the Poconos.

A tree of Canada and New England, red spruce (*Picea rubens*) occurs in scattered locations in northern and central Pennsylvania, but makes its best growth and is most common in the Poconos. Although the finest red spruce stands were harvested during the late 1800s, some excellent stands still occur.

The one to two-inch long immature cones of red spruce remain closed until autumn, when they turn a reddish-brown and the scales open slightly to disperse the winged seeds. The cones mature in one growing season. The seeds are consumed by several species of songbirds.

The red spruce forests in the Poconos are frequently intermixed with eastern hemlock and occasionally balsam fir. This makes a true boreal forest that supports plants and animals common farther north but unique to Pennsylvania. This is also the home for the state endangered northern flying squirrel.

Mistaken for young conifer trees, clubmosses are non-flowering spore-bearing plants common in Pocono forests. Growing to eight inches high, many species also have creeping horizontal stems. Ground pine or princess pine (*Lycopodium obscurum*), as seen here, has been used for Christmas decorations. A permit is needed to harvest clubmosses in state forests.

Tobyhanna Creek flows through the Austin T. Blakeslee Natural Area near the village of Blakeslee. Here the creek forms a scenic waterfall of a mere ten feet known as Tobyhanna Falls. The Pennsylvania Geological Survey has listed this area as one of the Outstanding Geological Features of Pennsylvania.

A mature hardwood forest and a dense understory of rhododendron grow along the banks of Tank Creek in the 400-acre Kurmes Preserve in Paradise Township, Monroe County. Several miles of hiking trails give access to this pristine natural reserve preserved by the Pocono Heritage Land Trust.

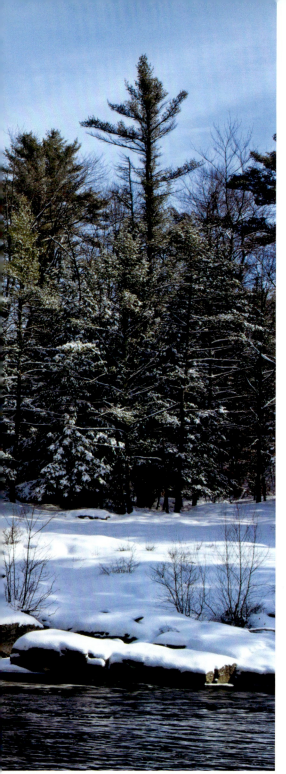

Most of the land now making up Tobyhanna and Gouldsboro State Parks and State Game Lands 127 was once part of a larger Tobyhanna Army Depot. This land was used for artillery training between 1913 and 1941. Soldiers hid behind parapets made of native stone while firing 75mm cannons.

Groups of parapets built between 1913 and 1914 can be seen along Route 423 and in Tobyhanna State Park. In 2007 William Beehla—grandson of the original builder—and a group of volunteers began restoring and rebuilding these long-forgotten structures that were once important to our nation's military training.

Another choice edible mushroom that appears at the end of summer is hen of the woods (*Grifola frondosa*, aka: *Poluporus frondosus*). In the Poconos, it is usually found growing on both live and dead red oak trees. It forms clusters up to twenty inches wide.

During warm summer rainstorms, the juvenile stage of the red-spotted newt (*Notophthalmus viridescens*) is seen walking about Pocono woodlands during the day. Called red efts, these juveniles will return to the water as adults—where they spent their larva stage—for the rest of their lives, never returning to land.

Resembling a piece of sea coral, beautiful comb tooth fungus (*Hericium ramosum*) is found growing on decaying beech and maple logs during August and September in the Poconos. It is reported to be a rather choice edible mushroom, but positive identification is always critical with any wild fungus.

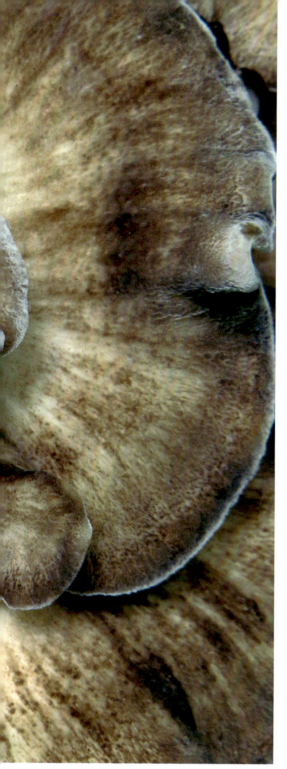

Blue cohosh (*Caulophyllum thalictroides*) is one of the first wildflowers to bloom in spring with rather inconspicuous tiny flowers. In late summer the bluish berries develop as the plant begins to die back. Native Americans used the plant's roots to stimulate labor in childbirth and treat menstruation and other "female ailments."

Pond Swamp—an acidic glacial bog on State Game Lands 127—resembles a scene typical of northern Canada with its tamaracks, red spruce, cotton grass, rhodora, and heaths. It is accessible only through a difficult and wet bushwhack. The Pennsylvania Natural Diversity Inventory lists it as an "Ecological Significant Area."

Early coralroot (*Corallorhiza trifida*) is often overlooked due to its small size and preference for bogs and wet thickets. Interestingly, this native wild orchid lacks chlorophyll and roots. It is totally dependent on underground fungus from which it absorbs nutrients through a coral-like rootstock that is actually a mutated stem.

Grass-pink or calopogon orchid (*Calopogon tuberosus*) can sometimes be found growing in wet meadows but more commonly in boreal sphagnum bogs in the Poconos. Although not endangered, it is rare enough that it should never be picked, and it will not survive transplant attempts to home gardens.

The short, carnivorous roundleaf sundew (*Drosera rotundifolia*) is almost always found growing in sphagnum moss. The sweet, sticky moisture on the half-inch round leaves attracts insects, which are then trapped, to be digested by the plant for nutrients. This plant is uncommonly circumboreal, being found naturally across the Northern Hemisphere.

The lower branches on black spruce (*Picea mariana*) often take root in sphagnum moss, forming a small circle of trees. A slow growing tree rarely reaching thirty feet high, it sometimes averages only one inch a year in height. A twenty-foot tree can be 200 years old, making it old growth.

The cones of black spruce resemble those of red spruce, but are smaller—one half to one inch long—and more rounded. They cluster near the top of the tree. In the Poconos black spruce grows mainly in sphagnum bogs and grows as far north as the tree line in Canada.

The banks of Rattlesnake Creek are lined with a thick and often impermeable stand of rhododendron for much of the over two miles that it cascades down the Pocono Escarpment. This dense shade keeps the water cool and clean, making this stream a valuable feeder stream for Brodhead Creek.

Humid summer air creates a layer of mist over the cold water of Brodhead Creek in Paradise Township. One of the finest and pristine streams in the Poconos, most of the creek's length is on private property, except for a half-mile section preserved on the 777-acre Paradise Price Preserve.

Rattlesnake Falls on State Game Lands 221 drops a total of twenty-six feet in two tiers. The falls is reached by a one-mile hiking trail that climbs up the Pocono Escarpment. Getting to the bottom of the falls requires a difficult climb down a steep embankment aided by a rope.

Common throughout the Poconos, pickerel frogs (*Rana palustris*) need unpolluted cool streams, sphagnum bogs, and ponds. The yellow patch near its hind legs is a distinctive field mark. Because this frog has skin glands that produce a distasteful secretion few snakes will eat this species.

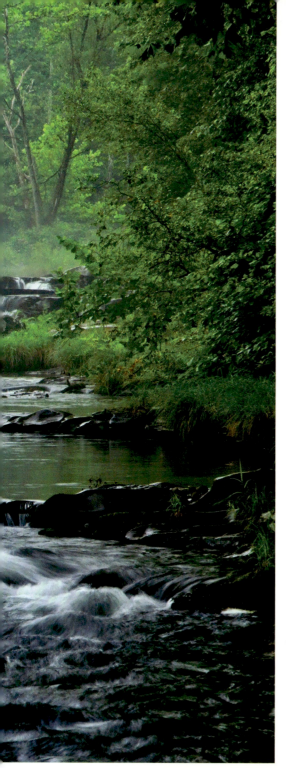

Spruce Swamp State Forest Natural Area in
Lackawanna State Forest, near Thornhurst,
contains all the boreal trees species native to
Pennsylvania, including red and black spruce,
balsam fir, and tamarack. Additionally, many
northern shrub species such as rhodora, Labrador
tea, Canada yew, and leatherleaf also occur here.

(Top left) Another high elevation in the Poconos is Big Pine Hill at 2,265 feet, in the Thornhurst section of Lackawanna State Forest. Scrapped bare by passing glaciers, the exposed summit has maintained its open pitch pine/scrub oak/ heath barren habitat through repeated fires and severe weather.

(Bottom left) Plants rarely reaching three feet high such as black huckleberry (*Gaylussacia baccata*) and lowbush blueberry (*Vaccinium angustifolium*) hug the ground on ridge top heath barrens like Big Pine Hill. It was in this habitat that the heath hen (*Tympanuchus cupido*)—a type of grouse— flourished before becoming extinct in 1932.

(Bottom middle) Between 1933 and 1937, the men of the Civilian Conservation Corps (CCC) camp known as Bear Lake Camp #140, in the Thornhurst section of Lackawanna State Forest, planted thousands of red pine and Norway spruce trees on the heavily logged land. Today these plantations provide a boreal forest habitat.

(Top right) A long-abandoned beaver pond along Hagen Run in Lackawanna State Forest is now an extensive moist meadow. Areas such as these were often the first settled in pioneer days, as the dense forest was already "cleared" and ready for livestock grazing along with a dependable water source.

Spring blooming yellow clintonia or bluebead lily (*Clintonia borealis*) is a member of the lily family named for NY governor and naturalist Dewitt Clinton. Growing in most acidic northern forests, the tiny three-quarter to one-inch flowers mature in late summer into quarter-inch extraordinarily beautiful bluish berries that are poisonous.

Crustose lichens form thin films on rocky surfaces. Ring lichen (*Arctoparmelia centrifuga*)—seen here growing in Lackawanna State Forest—produces annual rings similar to trees. Their age can be determined by examining these annual rings.

Closely related to flowering dogwood, bunchberry (*Cornus canadensis*) rarely grows to a height beyond ten inches. This native northern woody perennial prefers cool moist forest and bog edges in the Poconos. It is one of the few circumpolar plants being found from Greenland across northern North America to northeast Asia.

Due to the impenetrable conditions, very few people get to see the interior of a Pocono red spruce/hemlock/ highbush blueberry swamp. This is home to the black bear, snowshoe hare, and fisher. There are many false bottoms here where one wrong step can find hikers sinking in waist deep muck.

There are countless smaller glacial "boulder fields" in the Poconos as seen here in Lackawanna State Forest. What likely happened here was the passing glacier filled a depression with rocks and other debris. The melting glacial water washed away the soil and smaller stones, leaving only these rocks.

Growing in both dry woods and bog edges, the very showy fly poison (*Amianthium muscitoxicum*) blooms in early summer, displaying two to six-inch flower clusters. Its odd common name comes from the practice of using the pulp from crushed bulbs mixed with sugar to poison flies.

During most seasons Butler Run in Lackawanna State Forest is merely a small streamlet. However, after heavy spring rains it turns into a picturesque stream, yet is still too small and too seasonal to support fish life, except small minnow types.

The Commonwealth of Pennsylvania acquired scenic forty-foot high Choke Creek Falls in 2010 as part of a 2,650-acre land parcel purchase for Lackawanna State Forest through the efforts of a consortium of governmental and private organizations. The wild, pristine qualities of the area are now threatened by nearby massive power lines.

One of the newest additions to the Delaware State Forest is the former 486-acre Rock Hill Scout Camp. At its heart is pristine eighteen-acre glacial Rock Hill Pond, which the Pike County Natural Heritage Inventory classified as "Exceptional Significance." It is habitat for four plants of special concern in Pennsylvania.

The fearsome looking one- to two-inch long eastern eyed click beetle (*Alaus oculatus*), with its fake "eyespots," is completely harmless to humans, as the adult feeds only on nectar and plant juice. The larvae are predatory, eating grubs of wood-boring beetles. This beetle may be discovered in a home woodpile.

Confederate violet (*Viola sororia priceana*), once classified a distinct species (*Viola priceanais*), is now generally considered to be a color variety of common blue violet. Its natural habitat includes open woodlands and moist forested slopes along rivers. It can also be commonly found in shaded city parks and lawns.

The upper Lehigh River reflects the color of an autumn forest as it drifts along the northeast boundary of State Game Land 127. As the Lehigh River flows to meet the Delaware River at Easton it serves as the boundary between several counties.

After sluggishly meandering through miles of bog and boreal wetlands, Fritz Run emerges in a northern hardwood forest to become a tributary of the upper Lehigh River. At this point it even holds a small population of native brook trout.

In Dry Land Hill Parcel of the 3,412-acre Bear Creek Preserve, the hiker is rewarded to a magnificent view of the Lehigh River upstream from Francis Walter Dam. Preserved by the Natural Lands Trust, this protected area provides critical habitat for a myriad of wildlife species and is a priceless asset.

The meandering course of the Lehigh River carving its path through Lehigh Gorge State Park is dramatically displayed from a Scrub Mountain rocky overlook on State Game Lands 141. The park was established in 1980 after the Central Railroad of New Jersey abandoned its main line through the gorge.

Glen Onoko Run is a popular hiking area near Jim Thorpe on State Game Lands 141. An unmaintained trail follows the steep climb up Broad Mountain, passing several small cascades. The first major waterfall reached is twenty-five-foot high Chameleon Falls. This trail can be very slippery, with dangerous, steep sides.

Over thirty miles of the Lehigh River flow through steep-sided Lehigh Gorge State Park. In the early nineteenth century dams, locks, and canals were built along the river, mainly to transport anthracite coal. Severe flooding in 1862 destroyed the canal system and it was replaced with railroads.

Intense lumbering of old growth white pine and hemlock during the mid-nineteenth century occurred along the steep-sided Lehigh Gorge, followed by a massive forest fire in 1875 that ended all lumbering activity. Today the slopes have recovered as a second growth forest with a variety of hardwood and conifer species.

Forty-five-foot high Onoko Falls is the main destination when hiking along Glen Onoko Run. During the late nineteenth century a lavish hotel stood near where Glen Onko Run emptied into the Lehigh River. On weekends thousands of people adorned in their Victorian attire arrived by train to hike the glen.

The borough of Jim Thorpe, sitting along the Lehigh River in Carbon County, was founded as Mauch Chunk, but was renamed in 1953 in honor of renowned athlete and Olympic medal winner Jim Thorpe. During the nineteenth and early twentieth centuries the borough was an important railroad and coal shipping center.

During the holiday season the borough of Jim Thorpe displays a distinctive decorative style. Along with its nineteenth century architecture, an atmosphere is created in which the writing of Charles Dickens comes to mind. *Budget Travel* magazine awarded Jim Thorpe a top ten spot on "America's Coolest Small Towns."

The marble tomb of Olympian Jim Thorpe sits at the entrance of Jim Thorpe along Route 903. The borough was named in his honor. His casket rests on a mound of soil transported from his native Oklahoma and from the stadium in Stockholm where he participated in the 1912 Olympics.

The historic one-and-a-half-story, five-bay, red-brick Central Railroad of New Jersey Station in Jim Thorpe was built in 1888 in the Queen Anne Style. It now serves as a visitor center. On January 1, 1976, it was added to the National Register of Historic Places.

Today Jim Thorpe is renowned for its Victorian architecture, displaying a vast range of styles: Federalist, Greek Revival, Second Empire, Romanesque Revival, Queen Anne, and Richardsonian Romanesque. Several individual structures are listed on the National Register of Historic Places. The Old Mauch Chunk National Historic District was established in 1977.

One of the most famous architectural structures in Jim Thorpe is Asa Packer Mansion, sitting high on a hill overlooking the town. Built in 1861 for $14,000, the three-story, eighteen-room mansion was the home of Asa Packer: philanthropist, railroad magnate, and founder of Lehigh University.

The autumn forest palette along steep-sided Drake's Creek exhibits a Modernism influence. Each tree species displays a unique color and these colors can change as the season progresses. Autumn leaf color is also influenced by soil makeup, weather, and sunlight exposure.

The friendly downy woodpecker (*Picoides pubescens*) is likely the Poconos' most common woodpecker and is often confused with the larger hairy woodpecker. They frequent suet feeders and can at times become somewhat tame. However, they are not shy to scold when a feeder is being refilled and they have to wait.

There is no other moth or butterfly in the Poconos that can be confused with the beautiful lime-green colored luna moth (*Actias luna*). The 3.1–4.5-inch long adult with a four and a half-inch wingspan appears in early summer and lives no more than seven days before mating and dying.

Scenic Drake's Creek on State Game Lands 141 and Lehigh Gorge State Park cascades down Millstone Mountain to join the Lehigh River. This steep-sided creek valley is forested with a northern hardwood forest and a thick rhododendron understory, providing a cool, moist habitat for many bird and wildflower species.

The western shore of Little Mud Pond contains an excellent boreal quaking bog, giving the appearance of a lake hundreds of miles north in Canada. Some of the typical plants growing here are red and black spruce, tamarack, leatherleaf, bog, rosemary, cotton grass, and pitcher plant.

Little Mud Pond in Pike County is one of six natural glacial lakes protected within the Delaware State Forest. Except for some state forest cabins on the east and north side, the twenty-one-acre lake has a very wild appearance and harbors several plant species of concern in Pennsylvania.

Tamarack, highbush blueberry, and red spruce all add to the autumn palette in the boreal bog at Little Mud Pond. These bogs are best viewed from a boat, as walking on them can be destructive to their sensitive environment. They can also be potentially dangerous due to their false surfaces.

Growing across northern North America, Labrador tea (*Ledum groenlandicum*) is at the southern limit of its range in the Pocono Mountains. This short evergreen shrub grows only in cool boreal peat bogs with the flowers appearing in late spring. During the American Revolution a tea was made from the leaves.

Very few people ever get to see white-fringed orchid (*Platanthera blephariglottis*), as it only grows in undisturbed boreal sphagnum bogs that have not been influenced by human activity. Growing to a height of twenty-four inches, it produces several one and a half-inch flowers with a fringed lip. Its scientific name *blephariglottis* means "fringed-tongued."

In winter, the native snowshoe hare (*Lepus americanus*) is very much at home in the boreal bog, finding ample food and shelter. This is also an excellent place to find winter birds, such as crossbills and winter finches that have migrated down from the taiga of Canada.

Unlike the cones of other conifers, which hang downward with their scales slightly opened to release the seeds, the cones of balsam fir (*Abies balsamea*)—like all firs—grow upright. As the sap or "balsam gum" dries during fall and winter the cone scales fall off, releasing the seeds.

The common redpoll (*Acanthis flammea*) often visits the Poconos in large flocks some winters, while other winters it is totally absent. A bird of the tundra, in the Poconos it seems to prefer birch and other small trees. It frequents bird feeders and is very fond of thistle seeds.

The best and safest way to explore a Poconos bog is to visit the pristine 150-acre Tannersville Cranberry Bog, a National Natural Landmark owned by The Nature Conservancy. Expert naturalists from the Monroe County Environmental Education Center provide scheduled guided interpretive walks on the dry floating boardwalks.

The recently acquired Freytown section of Lackawanna State Forest contains some magnificent wetlands, as seen here along the East Branch Roaring Brook. In the early twentieth century, the Scranton Gas and Water Company purchased much of this land to flood for a proposed reservoir. The reservoir never materialized.

The red spruce forest growing in the Freytown section of Lackawanna State Forest looks much different than the hardwood forest off Tanglewood Trail. Both are growing in moist soils, but the hardwood forest generally grows in somewhat alkaline soil, while the red spruce forest grows in acidic soils.

All that remains of the thriving community of Freytown—established in 1830 in Covington Township, Lackawanna County—is the cemetery. In 1909, a water company purchased the town to build a reservoir. All the buildings were torn down, but the cemetery could not be flooded and the reservoir plans were cancelled.

Red-panicle dogwood (*Cornus racemosa*) forms hedgerow like thickets along moist forest edges. In spring the plant displays clusters of greenish-white blossoms and showy white fruit in late summer that is consumed by several species of birds. Because it is an attractive native plant it should be encouraged in home landscaping.

White Deer Lake is a natural forty-eight-acre glacial lake protected in Delaware State Forest. Quaking boreal bogs are on both the north and south ends of the lake. Because of high beaver activity here water levels fluctuate and stumps of drowned shrubs often appear above water level.

The chapel in Hickory Run State Park is one of five original buildings left of the once prosperous town of Hickory Run. In 1839, a town with six mills and a 150-capacity hotel began developing. Clear-cutting of the surrounding forest resulted in flooding and fires, ending the town.

Hickory Run State Park offers many scenic wonders, one being the twenty-four-foot high Hawk Falls, which gets its name from a family that owned the property. The falls can be reached by hiking the Hawk Falls Trail, a moderately difficult 0.6-mile trail that sometimes wanders through a tunnel of rhododendron.

Highly picturesque three-acre Hickory Run Lake was created along the creek of the same name. A small, fragile sphagnum bog occurs at the lake's inlet where cotton grass and other northern plants grow. This location is a good site to observe migrating spring warblers while standing on the forest edge.

In the wild the eastern painted turtle (*Chrysemys picta*) can live for more than fifty-five years. This is the most frequently seen turtle in the Poconos as it basks on the water's edge. They cannot be possessed in Pennsylvania without following specific Pennsylvania Fish and Boat Commission regulations.

Shanty Run flows for nearly two miles through State Game Lands 40 in Carbon County before joining the Lehigh River near Hickory Run State Park. This high quality cold-water trout stream possesses a wilderness character with its surrounding hemlock/hardwood forest and thickets of large rhododendron.

A 0.20-mile trail leads to Painter's Swamp in the Delaware State Forest. This impoundment enhanced by beaver activity is noted for its springtime birds and its autumn colors. Beaver, otter, mink, and waterfowl and herons can often be seen along the two-mile trail that circles the wetland.

No trip to Hickory Run State Park is complete without a visit to the sixteen and a half-acre boulder field formed by a continual freezing and thawing process in ridges near the field 20,000 years ago during the most recent glacial period. This unique geological landscape is a National Natural Landmark.

Tranquility prevails along McMichael's Creek in Sciota, Monroe County, after a February snowfall.

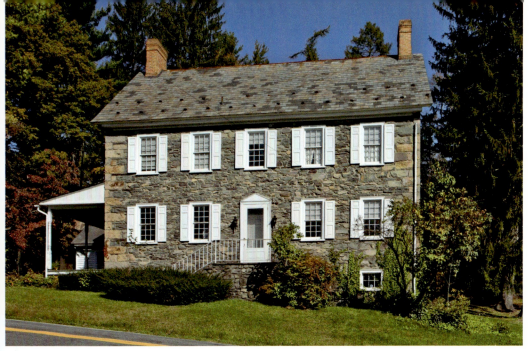

Fenner-Snyder Mill is along McMichael's Creek in Monroe County. Formerly a log structure, built in 1729, it served as a storehouse and advance post for 4,000 men during the 1779 Sullivan Expedition. The present stone structure built in 1800 is listed on the National Register of Historic Places.

The Fenner/Snyder/Robacker Homestead across the road from the Fenner-Snyder Mill in Sciota was built in 1805. It now belongs to Hamilton Township and is open occasionally for tours. Period furnishings can be viewed in several rooms.

The Old Mill, also known as the Fenner-Snyder Mill, produced flour and feed for livestock with its overshot wheel. At its height it employed two millers and continued milling until 1954. Its last owner, Karl Hope, presented it to Hamilton Township in 1974 "… for historical, cultural, and/or governmental purposes."

During the short days of winter a sunset brightens a Pocono meadow, giving a sense of warmth. It is scenes like this that make the Poconos so loved by so many people. Yet at the same time scenes like this are becoming endangered as the Poconos continue to change.

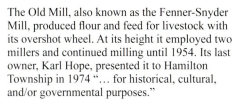

THE OLD MILL
SCIOTA, PA.

BIBLIOGRAPHY

Abramson, Ruby, and Jean Haskell. *Encyclopedia of Appalachia*. Knoxville, Tennessee: the University of Tennessee Press, 2006.

Allen, Peter, and Brian Cassie. *The Audubon Society Field Guide to The Mid-Atlantic States*. New York Alfred A. Knopf, 1991.

Amos, William H. *The Life of the Pond*. New York: McGraw-Hill, 1967.

Bancroft, Peggy. *This Land of Promise: The Promised Land Story*. Pocono Pines, PA: A Poconobook Series, 1994.

Barnes, John H., and W. D. Sevon. *The Geological Story of Pennsylvania*. Harrisburg, PA: PA Bureau of Topographic and Geologic Survey, 2002.

Behler, John L. *The Audubon Society Field Guide to North American Reptiles and Amphibians*. New York Alfred A. Knopf, 1979.

Barbe, Walter B., and Kurt A. Reed. *History of Wayne County, Pennsylvania 1798-1998*. Honesdale, PA: Wayne County Historical Society, 1998.

Bent, Arthur Cleveland. *Life Histories of North American Wild Fowl, Part One*. New York. Dover Publications, 1962. *Life Histories of North American Gallinaceous Birds*. New York. Dover Publications, 1963.

Bonta, Marcia. *Outbound Journeys in Pennsylvania: A Guide to Natural Places for Individual and Group Outings*. University Park, Pennsylvania: Pennsylvania State University Press, 1987. *More Outbound Journeys in Pennsylvania: A Guide to Natural Places for Individual and Group Outings*. University Park, Pennsylvania: Pennsylvania State University Press, 1995.

Brock, F., S. Fordyce, D. Kunkle, and T. Fenchel. *Eastern Pennsylvania Birding and Wildlife Guide*. Harrisburg, Pennsylvania: Pennsylvania Department of Conservation and Natural Resources, 2009.

Brooks, Maurice. *The Life of the Mountains*. New York: McGraw-Hill, 1967.

Brown, Scott E. *Pennsylvania Waterfalls: A Guide for Hikers and Photographers*. Mechanicsburg, Pennsylvania: Stackpole Books, 2004. *Pennsylvania Mountain Vistas: A Guide for Hikers and Photographers*. Mechanicsburg, Pennsylvania: Stackpole Books, 2007.

Chazin, Daniel D. *Hiking Guide to Delaware Water Gap National Recreation Area*. New York: New York-New Jersey Trail Conference, 1994.

DeCoster, Lester A. *The Legacy of Penn's Woods: A History of the Pennsylvania Bureau of Forestry*. Harrisburg, PA: Pennsylvania Historical and Museum Commission, 1995.

Felbaum, Frank et al. *Endangered and Threatened Species of Pennsylvania*. Harrisburg, PA. Wild Resource Conservation Fund, 1995.

Fergus, Charles. *Natural Pennsylvania: Exploring the State Forest Natural Areas*. Mechanicsburg, PA: Stackpole Books, 2002.

Fike, Jean. *Terrestrial & Palustrine Plant Communities of Pennsylvania*. Harrisburg, PA: Pennsylvania Natural Diversity Inventory, 1999.

Foster, Steven, and James A. Duke. *The Peterson Field Guide Series: A Field Guide to Medicinal Plants*. Boston, MA: Houghton Mifflin, 1990.

Freedman, Sally A. *Images of America: Delaware Water Gap the Stroudsburgs and the Poconos*. Dover, NH: Arcadis Publishing, 1995.

Freeman, Allen S. *Canadensis*. Paupack, PA: FOSI, Ltd. 1998.

Gadomski, Michael P. *Pennsylvania's Poconos...This is God's Country*. Reiman Publications, Country Extra, vol. 4, no.3 September 1993. *Reserves of Strength: Pennsylvania's Natural Landscape*. Atglen, Pennsylvania: Schiffer, 2013.

Geyer, Alan R., and William H. Bolles. *Outstanding Scenic Geological Features of Pennsylvania*. Harrisburg, PA: PA Bureau of Topographic and Geologic Survey, 1987.

Harrison, Hal H. *Peterson Field Guide Series: A Field Guide to Birds' Nests in the United States East of the Mississippi River*. Boston, MA. Houghton Mifflin Co. 1975.

Haywood, Mary Joy, and Phyllis Monk Testal. *Wildflowers of Pennsylvania*. Pittsburgh, PA: Botanical Society of Western Pennsylvania. 2001.

Hodgkins, Martha, et al. *The Field Guide to the Nature Conservancy: An Insider's Handbook to Places and Projects Around the World*. Arlington, VA: Nature Conservancy 2003.

IllicK, Joseph S. *Pennsylvania Trees*. Harrisburg, PA: Pennsylvania Department of Forestry, 1919.

Knapp, Vertie. "The Natural Ice Harvest of Monroe County Pennsylvania." College Paper. East Stroudsburg State College, 1972.

Kopczynski, Susan A. *Exploring Delaware Water Gap History: A Field Guide to the Historic Structures and Cultural Landscapes of the Delaware Water Gap National Recreation Area*. Fort Washington, PA: Eastern National, 2000.

Korber, Kathy, and Hal Korber. *Pennsylvania Wildlife: A Viewer's Guide*. Lemoyne, PA: Northwoods Publications, 1994.

Letcher, Gary. *Waterfalls of the Mid-Atlantic States*. Woodstock, VT: Countryman Press, 2004.

Lincoff, Gary H. *The Audubon Society Field Guide to North American Mushrooms*. New York: Alfred A. Knopf, 1981.

McCabe, Charlotte. *Down the Delaware: A River User's Guide*. Fort Washington, PA: Eastern National, 2003.

McCormick, Jack. *The Life of the Forest*. New York McGraw-Hill, 1966.

McKnight, Kent H., and Vera B. McKnight. *The Peterson Field Guide Series: A Field Guide to Mushrooms*. Boston, MA: Houghton Mifflin, 1987.

Merritt, Joseph F. *Guide to the Mammals of Pennsylvania*. Pittsburgh, PA. University of Pittsburgh Press, 1987.

Michael, Art. *Pennsylvania Overlooks: A Guide for Sightseers and Outdoor People*. University Park, PA: Pennsylvania State University Press, 2003.

Miller, Randall M. and William Pencak. *Pennsylvania: A History of the Commonwealth*. University Park, PA: Pennsylvania State University Press, 2002.

Mitchell, Jeff. *Paddling Pennsylvania: Canoeing and Kayaking the Keystone State's Rivers and Lakes*. Mechanicsburg, PA: Stackpole Books, 2010.

Newman, Boyd, and Linda Boyd. *Great Hikes in the Poconos and Northeast Pennsylvania*. Mechanicsburg, PA: Stackpole Books, 2000.

Niering, William A. *The Life of the Marsh: The North American Wetlands*. New York: McGraw-Hill, 1966.

Oplinger, Carl S. and Robert Halma. *The Poconos: An Illustrated Natural History Guide*. New Brunswick, NJ: Rutgers University Press, 1988.
The Lehigh Valley: A Natural and Environmental History. University Park, PA: Pennsylvania State University Press, 2001.

Osborne, Pete. *Images of America: Promised Land State Park*. Dover, NH: Arcadis Publishing, 2006.

Ostrander, Stephen J. *Great Natural Areas in Eastern Pennsylvania*. Mechanicsburg, PA: Stackpole Books, 1996.

Peterson, Lee. *The Peterson Field Guide Series: A Field Guide to Edible Wild Plants*. Boston, MA: Houghton Mifflin, 1978.

Peterson, Rodger Tory. *Peterson Field Guide to Birds of Eastern and Central North America*. New York, Houghton Mifflin Harcourt: 2010.

Pinchot, Gifford. *Breaking New Ground*. New York, Harcourt, Brace: 1947.

Pleasants, Henry. *A Historical Account of the Pocono Region of Pennsylvania*. Philadelphia: John C. Winston: 1913.

Poole, Earl L. *Pennsylvania Birds: An Annotated List*. Narbert: Livingston Publishing, 1964.

Rhoads, Ann Flower, and Timothy A. Block. *Trees of Pennsylvania: A Complete Reference Guide*. Philadelphia, PA: University of Pennsylvania Press, 2005.

Schneck, Marcus, and Glenn Davis. *Backroads of Pennsylvania: Your Guide to Pennsylvania's Most Scenic Backroad Adventures*. St. Paul, Minnesota: Voyageur Press, 2003.

Sevon, W. D., and Gary M. Fleeger. *Pennsylvania and the Ice Age*. Harrisburg, PA: Pennsylvania Geological Survey, 1999.

Stutz, Bruce. *Natural Lives – Modern Times: People and Places of the Delaware River*. New York: Crown Publishers, 1992.

Sutton, George Miksch. *An Introduction to the Birds of Pennsylvania*. Harrisburg, PA: J. Horace McFarland, 1928.

Thieret, John W., and William A. Niering. *The Audubon Society Field Guide to North American Mushrooms*. New York: Alfred A. Knopf, 1981.
The Life of Rivers and Streams. New York: McGraw-Hill, 1967.

Whiteford, Richard D., and Michael P. Gadomski. *Wild Pennsylvania: A Celebration of Our State's Natural Beauty*. St. Paul, Minnesota: Voyageur Press, 2006.

Websites

Audubon Pennsylvania. http://pa.audubon.org, accessed January 6, 2013.

Barrett Township Historical Society. http://www.barretthistory.org, accessed March 1, 2014.

Delaware Highlands Conservancy. http://http://delawarehighlands.org, accessed February 27, 2014.

Department of Conservation and Natural Resources: Commonwealth of Pennsylvania. http://www.dcnr.state.pa.us/index.aspx, accessed January 6, 2013.

First Presbyterian Church of Milford. http://www.firstpresbyterianmilford.org, accessed March 3, 2014.

Friends of Marie Zimmermann. www.friendsofmariezimmermann.org, accessed March 5, 2014.

Milford History. http://www.milfordpa.us/history.html, accessed March 3, 2014.

Pennsylvania Fish and Boat Commission: Commonwealth of Pennsylvania. http://www.portal.state.pa.us/portal/server.pt/community/pgc/9106, accessed January 6, 2013.

Pennsylvania Game Commission: Commonwealth of Pennsylvania. http://www.portal.state.pa.us/portal/server.pt/community/pgc/9106, accessed January 6, 2013.

Pennsylvania Historical and Museum Commission: Commonwealth of Pennsylvania. http://www.portal.state.pa.us/portal/server.pt?open=512&mode=2&objID=1426, accessed January 6, 2013.

Pennsylvania Land Trust Association: www.conserveland.org, accessed January 6, 2012.

The Pinchots and Milford: A Walking Tour. http://www.fs.fed.us/gt/local-resources/pdf/GTWalkingTour.pdf, accessed March 4, 2014.'

The Nature Conservancy: Pennsylvania Chapter. http://www.nature.org/ourinitiatives/regions/northamerica/united-states/pennsylvania/index.htm, accessed January 6, 2012.

The Nature Conservancy, Scientists Locate Natural "Strongholds" that Could Protect Nature in the Face of Climate Change. http://www.nature.org/newsfeatures/pressreleases/scientists-locate-natural-strongholds-that-could-protect-nature-in-the-face.xml, accessed June 8, 2014.

WJFF-FM 90.5FM: Radio Catskill, Audio Archive, Farm & Country, October 19, 2013, Helen Wade interviewing Dr. Mead Shaffer, http://www. wjffradio.org, accessed May 20, 2014.

The Times-Tribune. Erin L. Nissley. Local History: Ghosts on the Map. http://thetimes-tribune.com/news/local-history-ghosts-on-the-map-1.1570941, accessed March 15, 2014.

National Historic Lookout Register. Big Pocono Lookout. http://www.nhlr.org/lookouts/Lookout.aspx?id=56, accessed March 15, 2014.

Dorflinger-Suydam Wildlife Sanctuary. http://www.dorflinger.org/index.html, accessed March 18, 2014.

Foote, Knowlton, Ph.D. Blackeyed Susan (Rudbecka hirta L. http://www.nyflora. org/files/4812/9117/0362/NYFA_Newsletter_Vol_13_1_02.pdf, accessed March 21, 2014.

Nature Gate II. http://www.luontoportti. com/suomi/en/, accessed March 26, 2014.

Leonard, Bill, Jr. About The Ice Harvest. http://www.dgroff.com/tobyhanna. htm, accessed March 28, 2014.

Nabors, Susan, Kathryn Piff, Acey Lee, and Terese Gausman. Historic Stroudsburg, A Self-guided Walking Tour. http://beta. asoundstrategy.com/sitemaster/userUploads/site215/HistoricTour.pdf, accessed June 1, 2014.